Jamie's
FRIDAY NIGHT FEAST
COOKBOOK

MICHAEL JOSEPH

an imprint of

PENGUIN BOOKS

Dedicated to

DAVID MICHAEL DOHERTY

Jimmy's dad sadly passed away this year – he was a wonderful, witty, kind, hard-working man, and was always so proud of everything Jimmy, and his brother, Danny, did. He had a fantastic sense of humour and, as one of Jimmy's oldest friends, I always remember him and Jimmy's mum, Brenda, being such cool, patient parents, forever putting up with our antics as kids, teenagers and beyond.

Big love Dave xxx

CONTENTS

DEAR FRIDAY NIGHT FEAST-LOVING, FOOD-LOVING FRIENDS

· ·

Welcome to what I like to think of as the greatest hits of weekend cooking. Embracing incredible veg, fish and meat dishes from all over the world, this beauty of a book is all about the feasting. It's about family and friends, it's about sharing the love, and it's definitely about taking things that little bit further in order to wow and surprise your friends and family. I'm so glad you're here on this wonderful food adventure – not only are these recipes utterly delicious, they really push things to the limit, stir up emotion and knock people's socks off – exactly what you want from an epic feast!

Every Friday when I'm at work and shout to my team: 'It's the weekend!' there's always a mob of happy people squealing with excitement. For me, this not only represents the energy and pace of the TV show but also the food that you'll find on the pages that follow. It's food to get really bloody excited about. This is not a weekday cookbook and these aren't supposed to be humble, quick or perfectly balanced plates – they're 'hell-yeah!' recipes, blinged to the max, with a wonderful essence of eccentricity that takes them sailing up and over the bar to the next level. You'll notice that they're longer than my usual offering, and this is because they're not just meals, they're feasts! I've pulled out all the stops and gone to the effort of making everything from scratch – from condiments, salsas, pestos and pastes, to flatbreads, doughs and pastry – it's the full monty.

The pier is a phenomenally beautiful spot – it's where me and Jimmy grew up and it will always have a special place in both our hearts. I feel very blessed to present with Jim, who is an extraordinary fella. We've been side by side since nursery at the age of two, through primary and secondary school, to now presenting together with the aim of inspiring the nation to cook and to vote for a better food system. We're both extremely passionate about fighting to save food we're at risk of losing. It's been an incredible journey and a truly wonderful friendship – Jim is honestly one of the funniest people I've ever met. He's also a fine cook, farmer, zoologist, and someone who has travelled, seen and discovered more about the food industry, globally, than anyone else I know. The knowledge in that boy's head blows my mind! As a duo we just work – me with my cooking and Jim with his science and farming knowledge, and of course his famous builds – united through our love of food, people, family, friends, and yep – you guessed it – the weekend!

Choosing the recipes and photos that made the cut for the book really reminded me that the years we've spent making the show have been up there with some of the best years of my life. Also that the concept of *Friday Night Feast* is really kinda bonkers! We cook with, feed and interview A-list celebs 1.3 miles out at sea, slap bang at the end of the longest pier not only in the UK but in the world! Come rain or shine, we're out there in humble Southend-on-Sea, in the dinkiest little café, cooking up a storm – now, that's pretty nuts. But I absolutely love it!

A decent chunk of the recipes in this book are built around some of the most intimate and profound moments in our wonderful celebrity guests' lives, and are inspired by recipes, techniques and ideas from incredible chefs and cooks the world over, from street-food stalls and beachside shacks to family-run restaurants and even royalty! They're dishes that really mean a lot, and tons of research and effort goes into making them the very best they can be. To be able to meet and talk to these brilliant people about something that means so much to them, while cooking and sharing a meal, is truly one of the most exciting things about my job. From meeting my hero Mark Hamill, aka Luke Skywalker, and getting a cuddle from Joanna Lumley, to cooking with some super-talented musicians, comedians and actors I've admired for years.

Before I sign off, I have to pay homage to the amazing people I've worked with over the years – it's a big team, it's a big job, and getting all the kit and food to the end of the pier using the train (thanks, Southend Council!) is no mean feat. What I love most is the passion for food that everyone shares – from the film crew who are using the best cameras money can buy to capture those incredible close-ups of the food, to my food team who're busy prepping all of the dishes with love and care, to the hungry audience who are there to eat everything! Everyone at the pier is amazing, the atmosphere is beyond terrific and we always have such a laugh, which ultimately is what it's all about. I'd also like to say a huge thank you to you lot for tuning in, being curious and up for a laugh. Last series, we had over 12,000 of you request a seat in the café, and we can only fit in 30 people per show – it's humbling to see how this has become a Friday night favourite for so many. Enjoy!

Mark Hamill's

ROAST SIRLOIN & YORKSHIRE PUDDINGS

SERVED WITH EPIC BEEF-BONE GRAVY

• • • • • SERVES 6, WITH LEFTOVERS | TOTAL TIME - 6 HOURS 20 MINUTES • • • • •

This supercharged roast dinner will send your taste buds out of control. I've enlisted the force of science in order to get the Yorkshire puddings bang-on. It's a precise method, but the beauty is it's guaranteed to give you beyond brilliant results, every time. Make the gravy in advance, if you want to get ahead.

MARK HAMILL'S ROAST SIRLOIN & YORKSHIRE PUDDINGS
SERVED WITH EPIC BEEF-BONE GRAVY

YORKSHIRE PUDDINGS (MAKES 6)

4 large eggs

150g plain flour

175ml whole milk

50g beef dripping

GRAVY

2kg beef bones,
  with bone marrow

2 large leeks

2 red onions

2 heaped tablespoons
  plain flour

100ml red wine

100ml port

BEEF

2kg whole dry-aged
  sirloin of beef

olive oil

40g black peppercorns

3 sprigs of fresh rosemary

Ideally, make your Yorkie batter the night before. Whisk the eggs, flour, milk, 25ml of water and a pinch of sea salt to a smooth batter, then pop into the fridge overnight, removing when you preheat the oven for the meat (or, as a minimum, make the day you need it but leave to rest at room temperature for at least 30 minutes).

Preheat the oven to 180°C/350°F/gas 4. For the gravy, place the bones in a large roasting tray. Trim, wash and roughly chop the leeks, quarter the unpeeled onions, then add to the tray and roast for 45 minutes, or until golden brown. Remove the bones and veg to a large pot, keeping the tray of juices to one side. Top up the pot with 2.5 litres of water, bring to the boil, then reduce to a simmer for at least 2 hours 30 minutes, or until the liquid has reduced by half. Place the tray over a medium heat on the hob, then add the flour and stir well to pick up any sticky bits from the bottom. Pour in the wine and port, leave to bubble away for 1 minute, then gradually whisk in a few ladles of the stock, before tipping it all back into the pot. Simmer gently for a further 2 hours, or until you reach your desired consistency. Lift out the bones and strain the gravy, skimming off any fat from the surface, then adjust the seasoning, if needed. Keep aside to reheat at the last minute.

When you're ready, remove the beef from the fridge and leave to come up to room temperature. Turn the oven up to full whack (240°C/475°F/gas 9). Score the beef fat in a criss-cross fashion, then rub with 1 tablespoon of oil. In a blender, blitz the peppercorns, 1 tablespoon of salt and the rosemary leaves to a fine dust, then sprinkle and pat all over the beef. Place a large roasting tray on a medium-high heat, carefully sear the beef on all sides, then transfer to the oven. Immediately reduce the temperature to 180°C/350°F/gas 4 and roast for 50 minutes – this will give you medium-rare (cook for a little longer, if you prefer) – then remove to a board. Cover and rest for 30 minutes.

Turn the oven up to 220°C/425°F/gas 7. Divide the dripping between a 6-well deep Yorkshire pudding tray (8.3g per well, if you want to be super-scientific about it!), then place on the middle shelf of the oven for 5 minutes, or until the fat is smoking hot. Quickly but carefully pour the batter into the wells – each should be between half and three-quarters full. Immediately return to the oven and bake for 25 minutes, or until they have quadrupled in volume, are deep golden all over and sound hollow when tapped.

Carve and serve up the beef, adding a Yorkshire pudding to each plate, then drizzle with gravy (reheat, if needed). Delicious served with pinches of lemon-dressed watercress, horseradish and crispy roast potatoes.

CALORIES	FAT	SAT FAT	PROTEIN	CARBS	SUGAR	SALT	FIBRE
812kcal	51.4g	18.3g	44.2g	39.6g	8.8g	1.1g	2.4g

EPIC LAMB KEBABS

CHIPS, FLATBREADS & SUNSHINE SALAD

• • • • • • • • • • • SERVES 8 | TOTAL TIME – 1 HOUR 30 MINUTES • • • • • • • • • •

Cook the lamb until it's gnarly and almost burnt-looking, but still blushing inside – it's the contrast that's the thing of beauty. Hugged in a flatbread, topped with super-fresh sunshine salad, humble chips and a dollop of yoghurt – fantastic!

EPIC LAMB KEBABS
CHIPS, FLATBREADS & SUNSHINE SALAD

1.4kg lamb shoulder,
   bone out

2 cloves of garlic

3 lemons

1 heaped tablespoon
   dried oregano, ideally
   the flowering kind

100g feta cheese

150g natural yoghurt

½ teaspoon smoked
   paprika

CHIPS

1.6kg Maris Piper potatoes

1 teaspoon dried oregano,
   ideally the flowering kind

olive oil

FLATBREADS

350g self-raising flour,
   plus extra for dusting

350g natural yoghurt

SUNSHINE SALAD

1 red onion

1 large ripe tomato

1 cucumber

½ a white cabbage (400g)

1 tablespoon white wine
   vinegar

extra virgin olive oil

Preheat the oven to 200°C/400°F/gas 6. Score a criss-cross pattern into any fat on the lamb, then cut it into 2cm-thick slices. Peel the garlic and finely grate over with the zest of 1 lemon, then squeeze over its juice. Sprinkle over the oregano and a big pinch of sea salt and black pepper, rub all over, then cover and marinate in the fridge for 30 minutes.

For the chips, scrub the potatoes and slice into 1.5cm-thick chips, then parboil in a pan of boiling salted water for 6 to 8 minutes. Drain in a colander, leave to steam dry for 2 minutes, then lightly shake the colander to chuff up the chip edges. Divide between two baking trays, and season from a height with salt, pepper and the dried oregano. Drizzle each tray with 2 tablespoons of olive oil and toss to coat. Roast in a single layer for 35 to 40 minutes, or until golden and crisp, turning halfway.

To make the flatbreads, mix the flour, yoghurt and a pinch of salt together into a dough. Knead on a clean flour-dusted surface for 1 minute to bring it all together, then roll into 8 balls. Cover with a damp cloth. Thread the lamb slices on to a long, sturdy metal skewer to make one epic kebab (or split between two, if you prefer).

Preheat a large griddle pan or barbecue to high and cook the lamb for 15 minutes, or until dark and gnarly all over, turning regularly. Transfer to a large baking tray and roast in the oven for 5 minutes, or until just cooked through but still slightly blushing. For the salad, peel and coarsely grate the red onion with the tomato, cucumber and cabbage. Drizzle over the vinegar and 2 tablespoons of extra virgin olive oil, season to perfection, then toss together. Roll out the flatbreads on a clean flour-dusted surface into ½cm-thick rounds. Reduce the heat under the griddle to medium and – in batches – cook the flatbreads for 1 minute on each side, or until charred.

To serve, shave the meat off the kebab, drizzling over any resting juices (see tip below). On a plate, drizzle the feta with a little extra virgin olive oil. Put the yoghurt into a bowl and sprinkle over the paprika. Cut the remaining lemons into wedges. Serve it all in the middle of the table and let your guests get stuck in!

If you prefer your lamb crispy all over, put it back into the oven for a few minutes once shaved, or crisp it up in a dry frying pan over a high heat.

CALORIES	FAT	SAT FAT	PROTEIN	CARBS	SUGAR	SALT	FIBRE
877kcal	44.7g	19.3g	45.4g	78g	11.2g	1.9g	6.7g

Joanna Lumley's

AUBERGINE KUZI

TOPPED WITH TOASTED SULTANAS & ALMONDS

• • • • • • • • • • • • • SERVES 4 | TOTAL TIME - 1 HOUR 10 MINUTES • • • • • • • • • • • • •

Joanna has very fond memories of her childhood, much of which was spent travelling, as her father served in the 6th Gurkha Rifles. Designed to rekindle memories of Malaysia – a place she felt she belonged – this curry is something truly special. Serve with Roti jala and Sambal nenas (see page 23).

JOANNA LUMLEY'S AUBERGINE KUZI
TOPPED WITH TOASTED SULTANAS & ALMONDS

1kg mixed aubergines

olive oil

5cm piece of ginger

5 shallots

5 cloves of garlic

coconut oil

2 tablespoons brown
sugar

1 vegetable stock cube

2 tablespoons natural
yoghurt

20g sultanas

50g flaked almonds

2 fresh red chillies

KUZI MASALA PASTE

2 shallots

2 cloves of garlic

2 tablespoons paprika

2 tablespoons tomato
purée

1 tablespoon ground
coriander

1 teaspoon ground anise
seed (or 1 star anise,
crushed in a pestle
and mortar)

1 teaspoon ground cumin

4 tablespoons ground
almonds

Preheat the oven to 180°C/350°F/gas 4. Trim the aubergines, quartering any large ones lengthways and halving any small, then toss in a roasting tray with sea salt, black pepper and a drizzle of olive oil. Roast for 40 minutes, or until softened and golden (now's a good time to make the Roti jala batter – see page 23). For the paste, peel the shallots and garlic, then place in a food processor with the rest of the paste ingredients and blitz.

Peel the ginger and finely slice into matchsticks, then peel and finely slice the shallots and garlic. Place in a large frying pan over a medium heat with 1 tablespoon of coconut oil and fry for 10 minutes, or until softened and golden, stirring occasionally. Stir in the paste and fry for 3 to 5 minutes, or until smelling fantastic. Pour in 500ml of water, add the sugar, crumble in the stock cube, and bring to the boil, stirring gently. Add the cooked aubergine, reduce to a low heat and simmer for 20 minutes, or until the sauce has thickened.

Remove the pan from the heat and stir through the yoghurt. Toast the sultanas, then the almonds, in a dry frying pan until golden, while you deseed and finely slice the chillies. Scatter it all over the kuzi, and serve with Roti jala (lace crêpes) and Sambal nenas (pineapple relish – see page 23) – delicious!

CALORIES	FAT	SAT FAT	PROTEIN	CARBS	SUGAR	SALT	FIBRE
313kcal	20.7g	5.1g	11g	25.4g	21.9g	1.2g	2.6g

ROTI JALA (LACE CRÊPES)
WITH COCONUT MILK & TURMERIC

· · · · · · · · · · · · · · · · · MAKES 10-12 | TOTAL TIME - 20 MINUTES, PLUS RESTING · · · · · · · · · · · · · · · · ·

150g plain flour

1 large egg

120ml light coconut milk

1 pinch of ground turmeric

50ml vegetable oil

A delicious addition to any curry – work quickly, and remove from the pan while still flexible and before they take on too much colour.

In a bowl, combine all the ingredients except the oil, adding a good pinch of sea salt and 200ml of water. Mix until smooth, then leave to rest for 30 minutes.

Lightly oil a large frying pan, then place it on a medium heat. Spoon a ladleful of batter into a roti jala mould (you can buy these online) or squeezy bottle, and move in a circular motion to form a thin, lacy spiderweb pattern on the surface of the pan – keep the batter flowing. If using a mould, hold it 3cm above the hot pan and keep it full of batter for the best results. Cook for 20 to 30 seconds, or until slightly firm but not brown, then bang out on to a board (do not attempt to flip it).

Roll up, then repeat with the remaining batter, serving as and when ready.

CALORIES	FAT	SAT FAT	PROTEIN	CARBS	SUGAR	SALT	FIBRE
113kcal	6.6g	1.6g	2.2g	11.9g	0.3g	0.2g	0.5g

SAMBAL NENAS (PINEAPPLE RELISH)
WITH A HUM OF GARLIC & A CHILLI KICK

· SERVES 10 | TOTAL TIME - 10 MINUTES ·

1 small ripe pineapple

1 clove of garlic

2 shallots

3 fresh red chillies

2 fresh bird's-eye chillies

2 tablespoons brown sugar

1 lime

Liven up dishes with this refreshing but punchy relish. If you don't have a food processor, make it in a pestle and mortar instead for a slightly chunkier result.

Trim and peel the pineapple, cutting out the scraggy bits, then slice into wedges, removing and discarding the tough core. Peel the garlic and shallots, deseed the chillies, then pulse in a food processor until fairly fine. Pulse in the pineapple until fine, but still with a bit of texture. Stir in the sugar, pulse very briefly to combine, then squeeze and stir in the lime juice. Season to perfection with sea salt and black pepper, and serve.

CALORIES	FAT	SAT FAT	PROTEIN	CARBS	SUGAR	SALT	FIBRE
35kcal	0.1g	0g	0.4g	8.7g	8.6g	0g	0.1g

Alesha Dixon's

SPICY
PRAWNS

COCONUT MANGO SLAW & MINT CHUTNEY

•••••••• SERVES 2 | TOTAL TIME – 50 MINUTES, PLUS MARINATING ••••••••

Inspired by Alesha's travels to Mumbai, this incredible dish – also known as tandoori burani jhinga – has amazing layers of flavour from the punchy double marinade. To make my version really sing, I'm butterflying the prawns to give an even bigger surface area to suck up that wonderful fragrant spice.

ALESHA DIXON'S SPICY PRAWNS
COCONUT MANGO SLAW & MINT CHUTNEY

8 large raw shell-on tiger prawns

1 knob of unsalted butter

MARINADE 1

5cm piece of ginger

3 cloves of garlic

½ teaspoon chilli powder

½ a lemon

2 teaspoons mustard oil

MARINADE 2

80g hung curd (see tip)

10g roasted gram flour (bhuna besan)

2 tablespoons mustard oil

2 teaspoons red chilli paste

1 big pinch of kasoori methi powder (dried fenugreek leaves)

½ teaspoon carom seeds (ajwain)

½ teaspoon garam masala

SLAW

¼ of a red and/or white cabbage (200g)

1 little gem lettuce

4 radishes

2 sprigs of fresh mint

2 sprigs of fresh coriander

25g fresh coconut

½ a ripe mango

½ a lemon

extra virgin olive oil

MINT CHUTNEY

½ teaspoon cumin seeds

2 cloves of garlic

5cm piece of ginger

1 big bunch of fresh coriander (60g)

1 bunch of fresh mint (30g)

1 large fresh green chilli

25g unsalted peanuts

2 heaped tablespoons natural yoghurt

1 pinch of black salt

Peel the prawns, leaving the tails on, then run the tip of a knife down their backs and pull out the vein, meaning they'll butterfly as they cook. Place the prawns in a bowl. For marinade 1, peel and finely grate the ginger and garlic, then add to the bowl with the chilli powder, lemon juice, mustard oil and a pinch of sea salt. Toss together and marinate in the fridge for at least 1 hour. Meanwhile, mix all the marinade 2 ingredients together in a bowl with a pinch of salt. When the time's up, mix marinade 2 into the bowl of prawns, then leave while you make the slaw.

Finely shred the cabbage and lettuce and place in a bowl. Finely slice and add the radishes, then finely chop and add the herb leaves. Grate in the coconut. Peel the mango half, then finely slice half of it and add to the bowl, putting the rest aside for the chutney. Squeeze over the lemon juice,

drizzle with 3 tablespoons of extra virgin olive oil, and toss to coat. Taste and season to perfection.

To make the chutney, toast the cumin seeds for a couple of minutes, then tip into a blender. Peel and add the garlic and ginger, along with the herbs (discarding any tough stalks). Deseed and add the chilli, followed by the rest of the chutney ingredients, the reserved mango and a handful of ice cubes, then blitz.

Melt the butter in a large pan over a medium-high heat, then add the prawns with any remaining marinade and fry for 5 minutes, or until the prawns are pink and cooked through, turning regularly. Serve the sizzling prawns with the mint chutney and slaw. Delicious with a dollop of raita and poppadoms, if you fancy.

To make your own hung curd, simply strain 500g of natural yoghurt through a double layer of muslin and leave it to hang for at least 3 to 4 hours, or until drained completely. It will keep happily in the fridge for up to 3 days.

CALORIES	FAT	SAT FAT	PROTEIN	CARBS	SUGAR	SALT	FIBRE
705kcal	59.3g	16.6g	22.5g	21.8g	15g	4g	6.5g

John Bishop's
ULTIMATE VEGGIE LASAGNE

HOMEMADE HERBY PESTO & CRISPY SEEDS

••••••• SERVES 14 | TOTAL TIME - 3 HOURS 30 MINUTES TO 4 HOURS •••••••

Built from John's love of a lasagne cooked for him by his friend Jane, plus tips from his wife on his absolute favourite comfort food, enjoy this veg-packed twist on the traditional family favourite. It's got a hit of smoky aubergine for a turbo-boost of flavour, plus a super-fresh pesto topping I know you'll love. Delicious!

JOHN BISHOP'S ULTIMATE VEGGIE LASAGNE
HOMEMADE HERBY PESTO & CRISPY SEEDS

20g dried porcini
 mushrooms

2 onion squash
 (850g in total)

olive oil

1 teaspoon fennel seeds

dried chilli flakes

2 onions

2 carrots

2 sticks of celery

1 mixed bunch of fresh
 woody herbs, such as
 thyme, rosemary,
 sage, bay (30g)

100ml Barolo, or other
 red wine

2 x 400g tins of quality
 plum tomatoes

2 x 400g tins of beans,
 such as cannellini,
 borlotti, haricot

1 big aubergine (600g)

4 cloves of garlic

250g mixed mushrooms

500ml crème fraîche

100g vegetarian hard
 cheese

100g baby spinach

350g fresh lasagne sheets

100g Cheddar cheese

100g ripe mixed-colour
 cherry tomatoes

Preheat the oven to 180°C/350°F/gas 4. Cover the dried porcini with boiling water and leave to rehydrate. Halve the squash, then scoop out and wash the seeds. Drain and pat dry, then, on a tray, toss with a drizzle of oil, the fennel seeds, and a pinch each of chilli flakes, sea salt and black pepper. Chop each squash into 8 chunky wedges, then toss on a large tray with a little oil, salt, pepper and another good pinch of chilli flakes. Roast the squash for 1 hour, or until golden, adding the tray of seeds for the last 30 minutes.

For the ragù, peel the onions, carrots and celery, then chop it all into 1cm dice and place in a large casserole pan with 2 tablespoons of oil. Cook on a medium heat for 20 minutes, or until softened, stirring occasionally. Saving a sprig each of rosemary and thyme, tie the rest of the woody herbs together with string. Add to the pan for a few minutes, then pour in the wine and leave to cook away. Scrunch in the tomatoes through your clean hands, then pour in 2 tins' worth of water. Leave to tick away for 30 minutes, then drain and add the beans. Cook for a further 30 minutes, or until thickened and reduced, stirring and mashing occasionally, adding splashes of water to loosen, if needed. Season to perfection. Meanwhile, place the aubergine directly over a flame on the hob, turning regularly with tongs until softened and blackened all over. Place in a bowl, cover with clingfilm and leave for 5 minutes. When the time's up, remove the clingfilm, pour the juices into the pan, then halve the aubergine lengthways, scrape out all the flesh, and stir into the pan.

For the white sauce, peel and finely slice the garlic, and clean and finely slice the mushrooms. Pick and finely chop the reserved rosemary and thyme. Place a saucepan on a medium heat with 2 tablespoons of oil, add the garlic for 1 minute, then add the herbs, mushrooms and a pinch of salt and pepper. Cook until lightly golden, stirring regularly. Add the porcini and soaking liquor (discarding just the last gritty bit), leave to bubble and cook away, then turn the heat down to low, stir in the crème fraîche and cook gently for a few minutes. Remove from the heat, then finely grate and stir in half the hard cheese. To assemble, remove the herbs from the ragù, finely grate and stir in the remaining hard cheese, then generously spoon 2 ladlefuls into the bottom of a 25cm x 30cm lasagne dish. Drizzle over 2 tablespoons of white sauce, tear over a quarter of the squash, scatter over a handful of spinach, and top with a layer of pasta. Repeat 3 further times, finishing with the remaining creamy sauce. Loosen the edges with a spatula to push some of the sauce down the sides, then grate over the Cheddar. Halve the tomatoes, quickly toss in oil, and dot over the top, then bake for 45 minutes, or until golden and bubbling.

Leave to stand uncovered for 30 minutes, then serve with a dollop of Herby pesto (see page 31) and a scattering of crispy seeds. Good with a fresh, seasonal salad.

HERBY PESTO

1 big bunch of fresh basil (60g)

1 mixed bunch of fresh herbs, such as mint, oregano, flat-leaf parsley (30g)

100g vegetarian hard cheese

½ a clove of garlic

100g pine nuts, almonds, walnuts

extra virgin olive oil

½ a lemon

Rip the top leafy half of the herbs into a food processor. Break in the hard cheese, peel, finely slice and add the garlic and tip in your chosen nuts. Add a pinch of sea salt and black pepper and whiz until very finely chopped, then stir through 8 tablespoons of extra virgin olive oil and the lemon juice. Have a taste and tweak to your liking (this makes more than you need, so freeze any leftovers for tasty meals on other days).

CALORIES	FAT	SAT FAT	PROTEIN	CARBS	SUGAR	SALT	FIBRE
507kcal	35.8g	16.4g	15.3g	29.4g	10.1g	0.9g	6g

THESE VALUES INCLUDE BOTH RECIPES

GUNPOWDER LAMB

PINEAPPLE SALSA, COCONUT RICE & MINT DRESSING

The small investment in time you make to blend the perfect combo for the gunpowder spice paste is the key to success here. That contrast you get between the outer, dark, gnarly, spicy crust and the blushing, sweet, juicy meat inside is just incredible. Served alongside a feast of rice and outrageous pineapple salsa, it's a double YUM!

1 x 2kg butterflied leg of lamb or hogget, bone out (ask your butcher to do this)

olive oil

1–2 fresh mixed-colour chillies

GUNPOWDER SPICE PASTE (PODI)

2 dried red chillies

2 teaspoons ground turmeric

2 teaspoons fenugreek seeds

2 teaspoons coriander seeds

2 teaspoons cayenne pepper

2 cloves of garlic

2 tablespoons red wine vinegar

2 tablespoons vegetable oil

MINT DRESSING

1 bunch of fresh mint (30g)

1 lime

150g natural yoghurt

PINEAPPLE SALSA

1 small ripe pineapple

1 red onion

1 lime

1 bunch of fresh coriander (30g)

extra virgin olive oil

COCONUT RICE

3 teaspoons mustard seeds

2 mugs of basmati rice (600g)

2 fresh mixed-colour chillies

3 tablespoons creamed coconut

Start by making the gunpowder spice paste – blitz the dried chillies, spices and a good pinch of sea salt and black pepper in a spice grinder or blender until you have a powder. Peel and add the garlic, pour in the vinegar and vegetable oil, then blitz to a paste. Trim the excess fat from the lamb, then lightly slash the flesh all over with a sharp knife. Rub the spice paste all over, really getting into all the nooks and crannies, then marinate in the fridge for at least 2 hours, preferably overnight.

When you're ready to cook, preheat the oven to 200°C/400°F/gas 6 and a griddle pan to high (or you can use the barbecue for added smokiness). Sear the lamb for 20 minutes on the griddle, turning regularly to build up a gnarly crust, then place in a roasting tray. Drizzle with olive

oil and pop into the oven for a further 20 minutes – these timings are for blushing pink, but feel free to adjust to your liking. Remove to a board to rest.

Meanwhile, make the accompaniments. For the dressing, pick most of the mint leaves into a pestle and mortar, add a pinch of salt and bash to a paste. Muddle in the lime juice and yoghurt, then season to taste with black pepper. For the salsa, peel the pineapple and onion, then cut into wedges (removing the pineapple core). Blacken in a dry frying pan on a high heat, remove to a board, chop into rough 2cm chunks and scrape into a bowl. Squeeze over the lime juice, then finely chop and add the coriander stalks (reserving the leaves). Drizzle over 2 tablespoons of extra virgin olive oil, and season to perfection.

CALORIES	FAT	SAT FAT	PROTEIN	CARBS	SUGAR	SALT	FIBRE
929kcal	59g	10.8g	33.7g	75.9g	7.8g	2.7g	1.9g

For the coconut rice, place a 24cm non-stick frying pan on a medium-high heat with 1 tablespoon of olive oil and the mustard seeds. Pour in 2 mugs of rice and 3 mugs of boiling water and season with a pinch of salt. Halve the chillies lengthways and add to the pan with the creamed coconut. Bring to the boil, give it a stir, then cover and cook for 10 minutes on a low heat, followed by 5 minutes on a high heat – you're aiming for a crispy bottom. Once cooked, carefully turn out, just like a sandcastle.

Finely slice the remaining chilli(es), then scatter over the lamb with the reserved coriander and mint leaves. Take everything to the table, slice up the lamb and let everyone get stuck in. Delicious served with a seasonal salad.

ULTIMATE BRITISH BURGER

BRIOCHE BUN, PULLED OXTAIL, RED LEICESTER & GRAVY

What can I say? This burger is unique, outrageously delicious and an indulgence every human deserves to have once in their lifetime – the perfect cheese-topped burger, tender Worcestershire oxtail, and a dipping bowl of the most incredible gravy. Cook two burgers at a time so you can really take care of the timings, and make this one of the best gastronomic experiences ever.

ULTIMATE BRITISH BURGER
BRIOCHE BUN, PULLED OXTAIL, RED LEICESTER & GRAVY

600g minced chuck steak
  (16% fat)

English mustard

4 brioche burger buns

40g Red Leicester cheese

PULLED OXTAIL

1kg oxtail, trimmed,
  cut into rounds
  (ask your butcher)

2 red onions

olive oil

40g plain flour

Worcestershire sauce

1.5 litres quality
  chicken stock

½ a bunch of fresh
  flat-leaf parsley (15g)

BURGER SAUCE

2 gherkins

1 ripe tomato

1 little gem lettuce

100g natural yoghurt

Preheat the oven to 180°C/350°F/gas 4. Season the oxtail with sea salt and a generous pinch of black pepper, then brown all over in a casserole pan on a medium heat for 10 minutes, turning occasionally while you peel and slice the onions. Remove the oxtail to a plate, add 1 tablespoon of oil and the onions to the pan, and cook for 5 minutes, stirring regularly. Return the oxtail to the pan, stir in the flour to coat, then add 4 tablespoons of Worcestershire sauce and the stock. Bring to the boil, then cover and place in the oven for 3 hours to 3 hours 30 minutes, or until the meat is super-tender. Strain the gravy into a separate pan and put aside, then tip the meat and onions back into the pan. Once cool enough to handle, carefully pick through the meat, discarding the bones and any wobbly bits, then gently mix back with the onions and a splash each of gravy and Worcestershire sauce, being careful not to break up the meat too much. Pick, roughly chop and stir through the parsley leaves (reserving the stalks).

For the burger sauce, finely chop the gherkins, tomato, little gem and reserved parsley stalks, then transfer to a bowl, stir in the yoghurt and season to perfection. Shape the minced meat into four equal-sized patties, being quite rough so they're not too compact, then season the outsides with salt and pepper. I like to cook two burgers at a time to achieve perfection, so get two pans on the go – a large non-stick pan on a high heat for the burgers and another on a medium heat for the buns. Place two patties in the large pan, pressing them down slightly with a fish slice, then cook for 8 minutes in total, turning every minute and brushing with a little English mustard after the first turn. Put the gravy and oxtail pans on a low heat to warm through. When the burgers are almost cooked, halve and toast two burger buns in the second frying pan. Finely slice the cheese and place on top of each burger, add a splash of water to the pan, then cover with a lid or a metal bowl and cook for a further 30 seconds, or until the cheese has melted.

To assemble the burgers, spoon a quarter of the burger sauce on to each toasted bun base, sit a burger on top, spoon over 1 tablespoon of the pulled oxtail (save the rest for another day) and place the bun lid on top. Serve the gravy in a bowl on the side for dunking. Repeat with the remaining two burgers.

CALORIES	FAT	SAT FAT	PROTEIN	CARBS	SUGAR	SALT	FIBRE
686kcal	35.5g	17g	46g	44.6g	9.5g	1.9g	3.4g

Greg Davies'
THAI GREEN CHICKEN CURRY

BABY THAI AUBERGINES & THAI SWEET BASIL

· · · · · · · · · · · SERVES 8 | TOTAL TIME – 1 HOUR · · · · · · · · · · ·

Greg has always been fond of Thai cuisine, but found a real love for it after gigging there, especially for Thai green curry. Now, the base of any good curry is the paste, so it's worth the effort to hunt out all the ingredients. Just remember, a little goes a long way, so make a big batch and freeze it in portions for future use.

BABY THAI AUBERGINES & THAI SWEET BASIL

2 long fresh red chillies

600g chicken thighs,
  skin off, bone out

vegetable oil

2 x 400g tins of light coconut milk

4 fresh kaffir lime leaves

2 teaspoons palm sugar

2–3 tablespoons fish sauce

10 baby Thai aubergines

1 bunch of fresh Thai sweet
  basil (30g)

PASTE

2 teaspoons cumin seeds

2 tablespoons coriander seeds

2–4 large green Thai chillies
  (prik chee fah)

12 small green Thai chillies
  (prik kee noo)

4 sticks of lemongrass

6cm piece of galangal (or ginger)

8 cloves of Thai garlic

10 Thai shallots

½ a bunch of fresh coriander (15g)

2 kaffir limes

2 teaspoons shrimp paste

1 teaspoon ground white pepper

For the paste, toast the cumin and coriander seeds in a dry frying pan over a medium heat until golden and smelling fantastic. Pound to a powder in a pestle and mortar, then tip into a bowl. Trim the chillies (deseed if you like) and roughly chop with the lemongrass (use just the thick, lower part, discarding the outer layer), then peel and chop the galangal, garlic and shallots. Place it all in a pestle and mortar with 2 sprigs of coriander (stalks and all) and a good pinch of sea salt. Finely grate in the kaffir lime zest, then pound to a paste. Muddle in the shrimp paste, ground cumin and coriander, and white pepper (or whiz everything together in a food processor).

Deseed the red chillies, finely slice at an angle and place in ice-cold water, ready for serving. Slice the chicken into 2cm strips. Drizzle 2 tablespoons of oil into a large heavy-bottomed pan on a medium-high heat. Add 3 heaped tablespoons of the curry paste (save the rest for another day) and a splash of coconut milk, then fry for 30 seconds, or until smelling fantastic, stirring continuously. Stir in the chicken, then, after 5 minutes, pour in the remaining coconut milk and bring to the boil, stirring regularly. Tear in the kaffir lime leaves and simmer for 10 minutes.

Stir the palm sugar into the pan and have a taste; the curry should be slightly sweet, but not overpoweringly so. Add the fish sauce and taste again – it should be well rounded, salty with an underlying sweetness. Quarter the aubergines and add to the pan to cook for 4 to 5 minutes (regular aubergines will take longer, so cook until tender), then turn off the heat. Pick and stir in most of the Thai basil, then drain the chilli and sprinkle over with the remaining Thai basil and coriander. Delicious served with jasmine rice.

Look for more unusual ingredients in Thai supermarkets or specialist shops.

CALORIES	FAT	SAT FAT	PROTEIN	CARBS	SUGAR	SALT	FIBRE
228kcal	15.9g	8.1g	16.6g	4.9g	3.8g	0.4g	3.4g

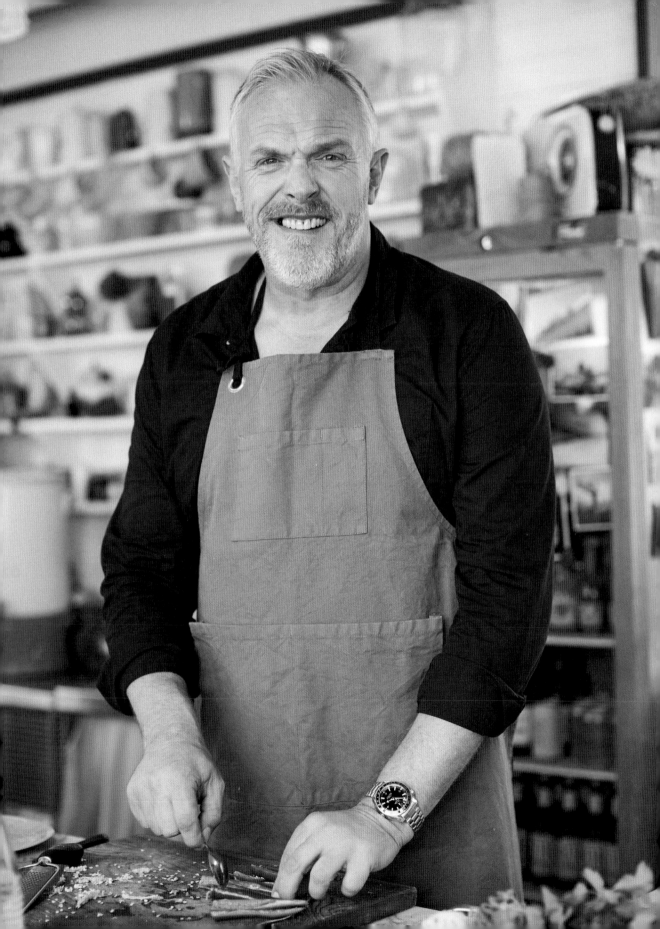

PEA & FETA FALAFEL-FRITTER WRAPS

EPIC GARNISHES & HOUMOUS WITH CRISPY CHICKPEAS

· SERVES 6 | TOTAL TIME – 1 HOUR · · · · · · · · · · · · · ·

Encapsulating the best of both worlds, this falafel-fritter hybrid gives you maximum surface area for optimum texture, which contrasts perfectly with the spongy-soft insides. Get your garnish game on – it'll really get the flavour party started – and encourage your guests to create their own bespoke wraps of deliciousness.

HOUMOUS

1 x 660g jar of chickpeas

½ a bunch of fresh
    flat-leaf parsley (15g)

100g jarred roasted peeled
    red peppers

1 tablespoon smooth
    peanut butter

extra virgin olive oil

1 small clove of garlic

1 lemon

QUICK PICKLE

1 pomegranate

1 red onion

1–2 fresh red chillies

1 cucumber

300ml cider vinegar

FALAFEL FRITTERS

½ a preserved lemon

1 bunch of fresh mint (30g)

1 large egg

100g feta cheese

100g fresh podded or frozen peas

2 heaped tablespoons self-raising flour

olive oil

GARNISHES

6 flatbreads

1 tablespoon red wine vinegar

2 little gem lettuces

100g natural yoghurt

hot chilli sauce

60g shelled unsalted pistachios

Tip the jarred chickpeas into a bowl (juice and all). To make the quick pickle, rinse the empty chickpea jar, then squeeze in half the pomegranate juice. Peel the red onion and very finely slice with the chilli(es), ideally on a mandolin (use the guard!). Slice the cucumber at an angle (I like to use a crinkle-cut knife), then add it all to the jar with the cider vinegar and a good pinch of sea salt and black pepper. Secure the lid and give it a good shake, then leave aside until needed (any leftovers will sit happily in the fridge for up to 2 weeks).

For the falafel fritters, remove any pips from the preserved lemon, pick half the mint leaves, then place both in a food processor with the egg, feta, peas and flour. Add 4 tablespoons of the chickpeas (without juice), then pulse until combined and set aside. For the houmous, spoon 2 tablespoons of the chickpeas (without juice) into a non-stick frying pan on a medium heat. Finely chop and add the parsley stalks (reserving the leaves), and add to the pan with 1 tablespoon of olive oil. Finely slice and add the jarred peppers, then cook for 5 minutes, or until the chickpeas are crisp. Tip the remaining chickpeas (juice and all) into the food processor (there's no need to wash it). Add the peanut butter and 2 tablespoons of extra virgin olive oil, peel and add the garlic, finely grate in half the lemon zest and squeeze in all the juice. Blitz until super-smooth, then transfer to a shallow serving bowl. Roughly chop the reserved parsley leaves, toss into the pan for 1 minute, then tip the whole lot on top of the houmous.

CALORIES	FAT	SAT FAT	PROTEIN	CARBS	SUGAR	SALT	FIBRE
467kcal	23.3g	5.4g	19.7g	43.9g	8.2g	1.7g	3.4g

When you're ready to cook, drizzle 1 tablespoon of olive oil into a large non-stick frying pan over a medium heat. Scoop in heaped teaspoons of the fritter mixture and cook for 2 minutes on each side, or until golden – you'll need to work in batches. Keep warm in a very low oven, as you go.

Now it's time to bring all the finishing touches together. Warm the flatbreads in the oven for a few minutes. Holding the remaining pomegranate half cut side down in your fingers, gently bash it with the back of a wooden spoon so all the seeds tumble into another bowl. Toss with 2 tablespoons of extra virgin olive oil and the red wine vinegar. Cut the lettuces into small wedges, pick and roughly chop the remaining mint leaves, and arrange both on a platter, with the quick pickle and houmous. Put the yoghurt into a bowl and ripple with chilli sauce, then bash the pistachios in a pestle and mortar. Take everything to the table and get stuck in.

Warwick Davis'
STEAK & STILTON PIE

BEAUTIFUL GOLDEN HERBY PASTRY

•••••••••• SERVES 10 | TOTAL TIME - 4 HOURS 35 MINUTES ••••••••••

In my mind, a pie like this with melt-in-the mouth crumbly pastry on the top, sides and bottom immediately hits heavenly status. For the filling, I'm using chuck steak and brisket, cooked until dark and caramelized. Let quality wine clean the pan, then bubble away for maximum depth and deliciousness. What a treat!

WARWICK DAVIS' STEAK & STILTON PIE
BEAUTIFUL GOLDEN HERBY PASTRY

1.2kg chuck steak
and/or brisket

3 heaped tablespoons
plain flour

olive oil

2 red onions

2 carrots

4 sticks of celery

4 fresh bay leaves

400g potatoes

400ml red wine

1.2 litres quality beef stock

100g Stilton cheese

1 large egg

PASTRY

400g plain flour, plus
extra for dusting

200g salted butter (cold)

4 sprigs of fresh rosemary

½ a bunch of fresh
thyme (15g)

½ a bunch of fresh
oregano (15g)

Slice the beef into 2.5cm chunks, then toss with the flour and a pinch of sea salt and black pepper. Drizzle 2 tablespoons of oil into a large pan on a medium heat, then brown the beef all over. Remove to a plate, leaving the pan on the heat. Peel and roughly chop the onions, carrots and celery. Add to the pan with the bay leaves and cook for 5 minutes, or until starting to soften, stirring occasionally. Remove to the plate with the meat. Meanwhile, peel the potatoes and chop into 1cm cubes. Pour the wine into the empty pan and leave it to reduce by half, then add the meat and softened veg back to the pan, along with the potatoes. Pour in the stock, bring to the boil, then reduce to medium-low and simmer for 2 hours 30 minutes, or until the meat is tender, adding splashes of water to loosen, if needed. Once cooked, season to perfection and leave to cool.

For the pastry, put the flour and a good pinch of sea salt into a food processor, cube and add the butter, then pulse until just combined. Pick and roughly chop the herb leaves, add to the processor with 100ml of ice-cold water, and pulse again until it forms a rough dough. Wrap in clingfilm and chill in the fridge for at least 30 minutes.

Preheat the oven to 170°C/325°F/gas 3 and lightly oil a 20cm loose-bottomed round cake tin. Roll out two-thirds of the pastry on a clean flour-dusted surface to 2mm thick. Loosely roll it around the rolling pin and unroll it over the cake tin, gently easing it into the shape of the tin. Patch up any holes and trim the edges. Spoon in two-thirds of the cooled filling (freeze the rest and serve as a stew another day). Crumble over the Stilton and brush the pastry edges with beaten egg. Roll out the remaining pastry so it's slightly bigger than the tin and top the pie, crimping the edges to seal. Make a small incision in the centre so steam can escape. Use any spare pastry to decorate the pie, if you like. Eggwash the top, then bake at the bottom of the oven for 45 minutes to 1 hour, or until the pastry is golden and the pie is piping hot. Leave to stand for 30 minutes, then serve up. Delicious with creamy mash, extra gravy and steamed seasonal greens.

CALORIES	FAT	SAT FAT	PROTEIN	CARBS	SUGAR	SALT	FIBRE
608kcal	35g	17.6g	25.4g	45.2g	3.6g	0.5g	3.4g

Martin Clunes'

MALLORCAN PAELLA

CHICKEN, PORK, CRAYFISH, TIGER PRAWNS, MUSSELS & SQUID

• • • • • • • • • • • SERVES 6 | TOTAL TIME - 1 HOUR 15 MINUTES • • • • • • • • • •

Igniting fond memories of happy childhood holidays for Martin, my take on a Mallorcan paella brimming with beautiful seafood is a real flavour extravaganza. Use a mixture of whatever lovely seasonal shellfish you can get your hands on.

MARTIN CLUNES' MALLORCAN PAELLA
CHICKEN, PORK, CRAYFISH, TIGER PRAWNS, MUSSELS & SQUID

6 large raw shell-on
  tiger prawns

1 pinch of saffron

1.2 litres quality chicken
  stock

3 chicken thighs,
  skin off, bone out

300g pork neck fillet

1 heaped teaspoon
  smoked paprika

olive oil

1 red onion

5 cloves of garlic

2 sticks of celery

6 crayfish

6 ripe tomatoes

400g paella rice

1 bunch of fresh
  flat-leaf parsley (30g)

200g squid, gutted, cleaned

200g mussels, scrubbed,
  debearded

200g jarred artichokes

150g mangetout

extra virgin olive oil

2–3 lemons

Preheat the oven to 190°C/375°F/gas 5. Peel the prawns, leaving the tails on, then put in the fridge. Place the heads and shells in a pan with the saffron, pour over the stock, then simmer on a low heat to infuse. Dice the chicken and pork into 3cm chunks, then toss with the paprika and a pinch of sea salt and black pepper. Place a large ovenproof frying or paella pan on a medium heat with 1 tablespoon of olive oil. Add the meat and cook for 10 to 15 minutes, or until golden, stirring occasionally, while you peel and finely chop the onion, garlic and celery. Remove the meat to a plate and stir the chopped veg into the fat in the pan. Cook for 10 minutes, or until softened, then return the meat to the mix.

At the same time, quickly drop the crayfish into the stock to cook for 4 minutes, remove with a slotted spoon, halve lengthways and place in a large bowl. Cut a cross into the bottom of each tomato, plunge them into the stock for 40 seconds, then carefully peel, deseed and roughly chop. Stir the paella rice into the meat pan to toast for a few minutes, then ladle in 1 litre of stock through a sieve. Add the tomatoes and simmer for 10 minutes, or until the liquid has reduced and the rice is nearly cooked, stirring occasionally.

Meanwhile, pick and finely chop the parsley. Run the tip of a knife down the back of each prawn and pull out the vein, meaning they'll butterfly as they cook. Slice the tentacles from the squid, keeping them whole, then open out the tubes and lightly score in a criss-cross fashion with a regular eating knife. Place the prawns, squid and mussels in the crayfish bowl with the drained artichokes, most of the parsley and the mangetout (roughly slice, if you like), then dress with a drizzle of extra virgin olive oil, the juice of 1 lemon and a good pinch of sea salt and black pepper. Poke and scatter the contents of the bowl into the rice, then place uncovered in the oven for 10 minutes, or until beautifully cooked. Scatter over the remaining parsley leaves and serve with lots of lemon wedges for squeezing over.

CALORIES	FAT	SAT FAT	PROTEIN	CARBS	SUGAR	SALT	FIBRE
642kcal	19.8g	3.9g	58.3g	66.3g	6.6g	3.1g	3.4g

BBQ BRITISH RIBS
HERBY POTATO SALAD & RADISHES

Cooked low and slow, ribs are a time investment, but if you want out-of-this-world flavour, you can't rush these things! My secret weapon is to smoke them for the last 30 minutes, kissing the meat with incredible depth and smokiness.

75g sea salt

2 tablespoons white
  peppercorns

6 fresh bay leaves

4 racks of pork loin
  back ribs (3kg in total)

150g radishes

BBQ SAUCE

225g HP sauce

300g tomato ketchup

170g English mustard

150ml Worcestershire
  sauce

100ml whisky

750ml fresh apple juice

200ml runny honey

POTATO SALAD

500g baby new potatoes

½ a bunch of fresh
  dill (15g)

1 bunch of fresh chives (30g)

50g pickled onions

1 eating apple

1 ripe pear

200g Greek yoghurt

1 teaspoon English mustard

> You also need:
> 1 small handful of
> whisky wood chips

Preheat the oven to 140°C/275°F/gas 1. Place the sea salt, white peppercorns and bay leaves in a pestle and mortar and bash until fine (or whiz in a blender), then decant into a jar. Rub 2 tablespoons of the flavoured salt over the racks of ribs (save the rest for another day), then transfer to two baking trays and cover with tin foil. In a 25cm x 30cm high-sided tray, mix the BBQ sauce ingredients together. Place all three trays in the oven for 3 hours, with the sauce tray at the very bottom, uncovered – keep an eye on it and add a splash of water to loosen, if needed.

When the time's up, remove the trays from the oven, adding a splash of water to each of the rib trays to deglaze. Divide 300g of the sauce between the two rib trays (cool the rest and freeze for another day), turning the ribs with tongs to coat. Place the ribs directly on the bars of the oven, with the empty sauce tray directly below. Put a handful of whisky wood chips into a metal sieve and set them alight. Once smoking, put the sieve into a metal bowl, place at the very bottom of the oven and smoke the ribs for 30 minutes, or until sticky and caramelized.

Meanwhile, scrub the potatoes, cook in a pan of boiling salted water for 15 minutes, or until tender, then drain and leave to cool slightly. Pick the dill, then finely chop with the chives and place in a large bowl. Finely slice the pickled onions, then core and finely matchstick the apple and pear. Add it all to the bowl with the yoghurt, mustard and warm potatoes, toss to coat, then season to perfection.

Transfer the racks to a board and slice into portions or individual ribs, drizzling any juices from the tray over the top. Finely slice the radishes and sprinkle over the top, then serve with the potato salad (and some napkins!).

CALORIES	FAT	SAT FAT	PROTEIN	CARBS	SUGAR	SALT	FIBRE
529kcal	27.8g	11.5g	37.5g	32.8g	19.5g	3.9g	3.4g

Simon Pegg's
LAMB TAGINE

HOMEMADE FLATBREADS & HARISSA YOGHURT

• • • • • • • • • SERVES 6 | TOTAL TIME - 2 HOURS 15 MINUTES • • • • • • • • •

Inspired by Simon's time spent on location in Marrakech, I've created this beautiful lamb tagine to transport him right back to the wonderful meals he enjoyed at the family-run hole-in-the-wall-style restaurants at the edge of the Medina. With brilliant spices and incredible, subtle aromas, it's seriously tasty stuff!

SIMON PEGG'S LAMB TAGINE
HOMEMADE FLATBREADS & HARISSA YOGHURT

1 large pinch of saffron

8 dried prunes (stone in)

2 onions

2 cloves of garlic

1 teaspoon ground ginger

olive oil

1 stick of cinnamon

750g diced lamb shoulder

12 mixed-colour
 baby courgettes

300g mixed-colour
 baby carrots

½ a butternut
 squash (600g)

250g couscous

2 cloves

2 tablespoons rose harissa

250g natural yoghurt

½ a bunch of fresh
 mint (15g)

In a small bowl, cover the saffron with 2 tablespoons of boiling water and leave to steep. Destone the prunes, place in a separate bowl and just cover with boiling water so they plump up. Peel and finely chop the onions and garlic, then season with the ground ginger and a pinch of sea salt and black pepper.

Place a tagine or large casserole pan on a medium heat with 2 tablespoons of oil, then add the cinnamon for 1 minute to flavour the oil. Add the lamb, season with salt and pepper, then cook for 5 minutes, or until browned all over, stirring regularly. Push the meat to one side of the pan, placing the cinnamon stick on top, then add the seasoned onion and garlic alongside. Cook for 5 minutes, or until softened and caramelized, stirring occasionally.

Gently scrub the courgettes and carrots, keeping them whole, peel and deseed the squash, then chop into 3cm chunks, and add it all to the pan. Pour in the prunes, saffron and all the soaking water, then top up with 200ml of water, and stir well. Bring to the boil, then cover and cook on a low heat for 1 hour 30 minutes to 2 hours, or until the lamb is tender and the veg are cooked through, stirring occasionally and adding splashes of water to loosen, if needed. Taste and season to perfection.

Meanwhile, place the couscous in a bowl, season with salt and add the cloves, then just cover with boiling water and a drizzle of oil. Pop a plate on top and leave for 5 to 10 minutes to fluff up, then use a fork to fluff up again. Fold the harissa through the yoghurt. Serve the tagine, couscous and flatbreads (see page 63) with the harissa yoghurt, finishing with a scattering of mint leaves.

CALORIES	FAT	SAT FAT	PROTEIN	CARBS	SUGAR	SALT	FIBRE
965kcal	37g	13.3g	41.4g	121.2g	21.5g	1.4g	3.4g

HOMEMADE FLATBREADS

MAKES 6 | TOTAL TIME - 20 MINUTES, PLUS PROVING

250g cornmeal

250g plain flour, plus
extra for dusting

1 x 7g sachet of dried yeast

olive oil

Mix the cornmeal, flour and a good pinch of sea salt in a large bowl. Stir the yeast into 275ml of warm water, then add to the bowl and mix to form a pliable sticky dough, adding a splash more water, if needed. On a clean flour-dusted surface, divide into 6 balls, then flatten each into a 10cm round, pushing your fingers into the top to give you a ripple effect. Place on a lightly oiled tray, cover with a clean damp tea towel and leave to prove for 45 minutes. Working in batches, drizzle a little oil into a large non-stick frying pan on a medium heat. Once hot, cook a few dough rounds for 2 to 3 minutes on each side, or until golden and perfectly charred, then repeat, topping up the oil between batches, if needed.

CALORIES	FAT	SAT FAT	PROTEIN	CARBS	SUGAR	SALT	FIBRE
360kcal	8.9g	1.1g	8.2g	62.8g	0.6g	0.3g	2.2g

Johnny Vegas'
FILLET STEAK
FLAMBÉ

MUSTARDY MUSHROOM SAUCE & PEPPER SPRINKLE

•••••••• SERVES 2 | TOTAL TIME – 15 MINUTES, PLUS MARINATING ••••••••

Johnny fell in love with a dish like this while filming in Cape Town. If you're looking for something to cook for a super-special occasion, it definitely has the wow factor. It's certainly not something you'd eat every day and is quite cheffy in method, but utterly joyful to eat. Do try flambéing – it adds an amazing depth of flavour.

JOHNNY VEGAS' FILLET STEAK FLAMBÉ
MUSTARDY MUSHROOM SAUCE & PEPPER SPRINKLE

1 sprig of fresh rosemary

2 sprigs of fresh thyme

1 teaspoon red wine vinegar

olive oil

2 x 150g centre-cut fillet steaks, ideally 2.5cm thick

100g chestnut mushrooms

½ a bunch of fresh flat-leaf parsley (15g)

20g unsalted butter

10ml brandy

50ml red wine

100ml single cream

1 teaspoon wholegrain or French mustard

1 teaspoon English mustard

PEPPER SPRINKLE

¼ of a red pepper

¼ of an orange pepper

¼ of a yellow pepper

extra virgin olive oil

Strip the rosemary and thyme into a pestle and mortar with a good pinch of black pepper, bash to a paste, then muddle in the red wine vinegar and 1 tablespoon of olive oil. Rub all over the steaks and leave to marinate for 30 minutes. Deseed and finely dice the peppers, then dress with extra virgin olive oil and put aside. Quarter the mushrooms, then pick and finely chop the parsley leaves. Get all the other ingredients measured out and ready to go, as you want everything to happen within 6 minutes once the steaks hit the pan – read to the end of the next paragraph before you start cooking so you know what's coming.

Place a large frying pan on a high heat to get screaming hot. Brush the herbs off the steaks, then place the steaks in the pan with a drizzle of olive oil and the butter. Cook for 6 minutes in total, turning regularly and keeping them moving in the pan, making sure to sear the edges and baste with the juices, as you go. Within this time, as soon as the butter turns dark golden and the steak has good colour and character, add the mushrooms and a pinch of salt and pepper, jiggling the pan to keep things moving. Pour in the brandy, then carefully tilt the pan to catch the flame (or light with a long match) and let it flambé – stand back! When the flames subside, add the red wine and reduce by half (if you need to put the flame out, swiftly place a large metal lid over the pan). Drizzle in the cream, turning the steaks in the sauce until they are nicely coated (briefly remove the steaks from the pan at this stage if your sauce is taking a while to reduce, to avoid overcooking).

Sprinkle over the parsley, then stir through the mustards. Slice the steaks in half, place on a warmed plate and drizzle with the sauce, then scatter over the dressed pepper sprinkle and tuck in. Delicious served with shoestring fries.

CALORIES	FAT	SAT FAT	PROTEIN	CARBS	SUGAR	SALT	FIBRE
581kcal	43.7g	19g	16.9g	5g	4.4g	1.6g	2.4g

Fearne Cotton's
MEXICAN
FISH TACOS

CHARRED PINEAPPLE SALSA & GUACAMOLE

· · · · · · · · · · · SERVES 4 | TOTAL TIME – 1 HOUR 25 MINUTES · · · · · · · · · · ·

Fearne first enjoyed fish tacos like these on holiday in Mexico with her best friend Lolly, so I've set out to recreate that vibe for her here. Served with all the trimmings – fresh guacamole, sweet and spicy pineapple salsa, garlicky soured cream and a jalapeño-spiked cabbage slaw – this is to die for.

FEARNE COTTON'S MEXICAN FISH TACOS

CHARRED PINEAPPLE SALSA & GUACAMOLE

1 bulb of garlic

½ a red cabbage (400g)

1 fresh green jalapeño chilli

1 tablespoon red wine vinegar

150g soured cream or natural yoghurt

1 lime

4 sprigs of fresh flat-leaf parsley

4–8 flour tortillas

1 x 400g tin of cannellini beans

olive oil

4 x 200g haddock fillets, skin on, scaled, pin-boned

1 lemon

PINEAPPLE SALSA

1 small fresh pineapple

1 small red onion

½ a bunch of fresh mint (15g)

2 fresh mixed-colour chillies

2 limes

extra virgin olive oil

GUACAMOLE

½ a small red onion

2 spring onions

1–2 fresh red chillies

2 ripe tomatoes

3 ripe avocados

½ a bunch of fresh mint (15g)

1 lime

Preheat the oven to 180°C/350°F/gas 4. Place the whole garlic bulb in the oven for 1 hour, or until softened, then remove. To make the pineapple salsa, trim and peel the pineapple, cutting out any brown scraggy bits, then slice into wedges, removing and discarding the core. Dry fry in a large frying pan over a medium heat for around 4 minutes, or until gnarly and charred, turning occasionally. Finely chop, then place in a bowl with all the lovely juices. Peel the onion, pick the mint leaves, then finely chop with the chillies (deseed if you like) and scrape into the bowl. Squeeze in the lime juice, drizzle with extra virgin olive oil, then taste and season to perfection with sea salt and black pepper, and put aside.

For the guacamole, peel the red onion, trim the spring onions, then roughly chop with the chillies (deseed if you like) on a large chopping board. Halve, deseed and add the tomatoes, destone the avocados and scoop over the flesh, then pick over most of the mint leaves. Chop and mix it all together until fine and combined, then squeeze over the lime juice and drizzle with 1 tablespoon of extra virgin olive oil. Season to perfection, giving it one final chop.

Very finely slice the red cabbage on a mandolin (use the guard!). Finely slice the jalapeño, then scrunch it all in a bowl with the vinegar to make a slaw. Squeeze the roasted garlic cloves out of their skins, then mash and fold it through the soured cream. Squeeze in the lime juice, add a drizzle of extra virgin olive oil, then season to perfection. Pick, finely chop and stir in the parsley leaves. Wrap the tortillas in tin foil and warm them in the cooling oven.

Drain the cannellini beans and put them into a frying pan on a medium-high heat for 5 to 7 minutes, or until they start to pop and blister. Place in a bowl and keep warm. Wipe the pan out and return it to a medium heat with a splash of olive oil. Season the haddock fillets and finely grate over the lemon zest, then cook skin side down for 4 minutes, pressing down lightly with a fish slice. Turn over for a further 3 minutes, or until slightly golden and just cooked.

Divide up the tortillas and top each with a spoonful of guacamole and slaw. Flake over the fish, then top with the pineapple salsa, garlicky soured cream and crispy beans. Pick, chop and scatter over the remaining mint, and serve with extra sliced chilli and lime wedges, if you like.

CALORIES	FAT	SAT FAT	PROTEIN	CARBS	SUGAR	SALT	FIBRE
751kcal	26.3g	4.7g	56.4g	72g	18g	0.9g	14.8g

CHICKEN KATSU CURRY

COCONUT RICE & ZINGY PICKLES

4 x 150g skinless boneless chicken breasts

250ml buttermilk

2 heaped teaspoons medium curry powder

2 cloves of garlic

120g panko breadcrumbs

1 mug of basmati rice (300g)

25g creamed coconut

2 litres vegetable oil, for frying

SAUCE

1 onion

2 cloves of garlic

5cm piece of ginger

1 medium carrot

1 bunch of fresh coriander (30g)

olive oil

1 teaspoon each garam masala, medium curry powder, ground turmeric

2 heaped tablespoons plain flour

1 heaped teaspoon mango chutney

PICKLE

1 red onion

1 lemon

1 fresh red chilli

Press down firmly with the palm of your hand to slightly flatten each chicken breast. Place them in a bowl, pour over the buttermilk, add the curry powder and a pinch of sea salt, crush in the garlic, then toss to coat. Cover and marinate in the fridge for at least 2 hours, but preferably overnight. When the time's up, sprinkle the breadcrumbs on to a tray. Remove the chicken from the buttermilk, shake off the excess, then turn in the breadcrumbs, pressing down to make them stick and flatten them a little more. Keep in the fridge until you're ready to cook.

For the sauce, peel the onion, garlic, ginger and carrot, then finely chop with the coriander stalks (reserving the leaves). Fry in a large pan on a medium-low heat with 1 tablespoon of olive oil and the spices for 15 minutes, or until starting to caramelize, stirring regularly. Stir in the flour, then the mango chutney. Pour in 800ml of boiling water and leave to blip away for 15 minutes, or until reduced to a nice sauce consistency, stirring occasionally. Taste, season and add more mango chutney, if needed.

Meanwhile, place 1 mug of rice in a medium pan with 2 mugs of boiling water and a good pinch of salt. Break in the creamed coconut and mix together. Bring to the boil, stir, then put the lid on and simmer for 10 minutes, or until the water has evaporated. Turn the heat off and leave with the lid on. Make a quick pickle by peeling and very finely slicing the red onion. Place in a bowl, finely grate in the lemon zest, squeeze in the juice and add a good pinch of salt. Deseed and finely slice the chilli and add to the bowl, then mix up.

Just under half fill a large sturdy pan with vegetable oil – the oil should be 8cm deep, but never fill your pan more than half full – and place on a medium-high heat. Use a thermometer to tell when it's ready (170°C), or add a piece of potato and wait until it turns golden – that's the sign that it's ready to go. Carefully lower the chicken into the oil, fry for 8 minutes, or until golden and cooked through, then drain on kitchen paper. Alternatively, drizzle 2 tablespoons of olive oil into a large, cold non-stick frying pan on a medium heat. Cook the chicken for 10 minutes, or until golden and cooked through, turning after 6 minutes and drizzling with an extra 2 tablespoons of oil as you turn.

To serve, put a quarter of the rice into a small bowl, press to compact and turn out on to a plate, then repeat with the other portions. Place the chicken next to the rice, cover with the sauce, then sprinkle over the pickle and the coriander leaves.

CALORIES	FAT	SAT FAT	PROTEIN	CARBS	SUGAR	SALT	FIBRE
886kcal	30.9g	7.5g	49.2g	111.5g	8.7g	1.5g	3.1g

ASHLEY JENSEN'S UMBRIAN PASTA

FRESH PORCINI, TRUFFLE & THYME

Having fallen in love with Italian food and culture while spending time in rural Umbria, for Ashley this dish is a total celebration of the purity of Umbrian food which she speaks so fondly of. The rustic unevenness of the pasta shape — umbricelli — is all part of the joy, so there's no need to worry about being too precise. Have fun!

½ x Royal pasta dough (see page 244)

Tipo 00 flour, for dusting

2 cloves of garlic

3 fresh porcini mushrooms (200g in total)

1 whole Umbrian truffle (15g)

extra virgin olive oil

2 sprigs of fresh thyme

2 anchovy fillets in oil

20g unsalted butter

20g Grana Padano cheese

Make the Royal pasta dough (see page 244). Once it's relaxed for 30 minutes, simply tear off 1cm balls of dough and, on a clean surface, roll them out into very thin 30cm sausage shapes, then place on a floured tray. The pasta will seem very thin at this stage, but don't worry it will puff up as it cooks.

Peel the garlic and put the whole cloves into a large pan of boiling salted water for 2 minutes (this will make the garlic creamy), then scoop out and finely chop, leaving the water on the heat. Clean and quarter the mushrooms, then very finely slice the truffle. Drizzle 2 tablespoons of extra virgin olive oil into a cold pan, place on a medium heat, then add the garlic, strip in the thyme leaves and scatter in most of the truffle and the porcini. Toss occasionally over the heat while you carefully add the pasta to the boiling water to cook for 4½ minutes (if you've left the pasta to dry out, it will take a little longer).

Add the anchovies to the porcini pan — they'll melt in — and toss together, then add a little pasta water to emulsify into a lovely mushroom sauce. Remove from the heat and stir in the butter. Using tongs, drag the pasta straight into the porcini pan, taking a little cooking water with it. Toss together, then finely grate in the cheese, and toss again. Scatter over the remaining truffle, season to perfection with sea salt and black pepper, and finish with a drizzle of extra virgin olive oil. Simply delicious!

CALORIES	FAT	SAT FAT	PROTEIN	CARBS	SUGAR	SALT	FIBRE
900kcal	47.6g	14.6g	33.5g	86.2g	1.9g	0.9g	4.5g

BRILLIANT VEGGIE BURGER

SPICED VEGAN MAYO & CRISPY ONION RINGS

•••••••••••••• SERVES 4 | TOTAL TIME – 1 HOUR 20 MINUTES ••••••••••••

I love this recipe – whether you're a hardcore vegan or just enjoying a meat-free meal, I know this will hit the spot. The patties are super-simple to make, and I've teamed them with spiced mayo and onion rings for an absolute treat of a burger. Of course, feel free to vary the toppings based on your own favourites. Enjoy!

BRILLIANT VEGGIE BURGER
SPICED VEGAN MAYO & CRISPY ONION RINGS

200g frozen sweetcorn

400g mixed frozen peas
and broad beans

½ a bunch of fresh
coriander (15g)

75g plain flour, plus extra
for dusting

1 pinch of ground cumin

1 teaspoon cayenne pepper

1 tablespoon sesame seeds

1 tablespoon sunflower
seeds

olive oil

½ an iceberg lettuce

2 ripe tomatoes

2 sprigs of fresh basil

2 gherkins

1 ripe avocado

1 lime

4 large quality burger buns

1 punnet of cress

tomato ketchup

Place the frozen veg in a food processor and let them defrost for around 15 minutes. Add the coriander (stalks and all), flour, cumin and cayenne, season well with sea salt and black pepper, then blitz to a rough paste. Pulse in the sesame and sunflower seeds until combined. Divide the mixture and shape into 4 equal-sized patties, roughly 2cm thick. Place on a lightly flour-dusted tray, turning them in the flour to coat. Firm up in the freezer for 10 minutes, then transfer to the fridge. Preheat the oven to 160°C/325°F/gas 3, while you make the vegan mayo and onion rings (see page 81).

When you're ready, cook the burgers in 1 tablespoon of oil in a large frying pan on a medium heat for 10 to 12 minutes, or until golden and cooked through, turning halfway and pressing down with a fish slice to get them nice and crispy. Transfer to a baking tray, then pop into the oven while you prepare the remaining ingredients. Finely shred the lettuce and mix with half the vegan mayo (keep the rest in the fridge for up to 2 days). Slice the tomatoes and place on a plate lined with kitchen paper. Sprinkle over a little salt and pick over the basil leaves. Top with another piece of kitchen paper and pat lightly to remove any excess water. Slice the gherkins lengthways, then halve and destone the avocado. Scoop out the flesh, cut into slices, then squeeze over the lime juice. Halve the burger buns and toast on a hot griddle pan or under the grill.

Once ready, pile the dressed lettuce and sliced tomatoes and basil on to the burger bun bases. Pop the burgers on top, snip over the cress, then layer over the avocado, gherkins and crispy onion rings. Add a good squeeze of ketchup to the burger bun lids, place them on top, squeezing down gently, then tuck in.

CALORIES	FAT	SAT FAT	PROTEIN	CARBS	SUGAR	SALT	FIBRE
425kcal	13.2g	2.4g	16.8g	61.4g	7.8g	1.1g	8.4g

SPICED VEGAN MAYO

2 spring onions

½ a fresh red chilli

½ a clove of garlic

2 heaped tablespoons
jarred chickpeas

1 teaspoon English mustard

1½ tablespoons sun-dried
tomato paste

1 splash of brandy

1 lemon

extra virgin olive oil

Trim and roughly chop the spring onions and chilli (deseeded if you like) and place in a blender. Peel and add the garlic, along with the chickpeas, mustard, tomato paste, brandy, lemon juice and a good pinch of sea salt and black pepper. Blitz well to combine, then, with the blender still running, slowly pour in 4 to 5 tablespoons of extra virgin olive oil until smooth and the same consistency as mayonnaise.

CALORIES	FAT	SAT FAT	PROTEIN	CARBS	SUGAR	SALT	FIBRE
123kcal	12.3g	1.8g	1g	2.2g	0.5g	0.6g	0.5g

CRISPY ONION RINGS

1 large onion

2 tablespoons red
wine vinegar

120g self-raising flour,
plus extra for dusting

½ teaspoon baking powder

200ml cold golden
ale or IPA

600ml sunflower or
sunseed oil, for frying

Peel the onion and slice horizontally into 2cm-wide rounds. Separate into rings, then place in a bowl with the vinegar and a pinch of sea salt. Leave for 5 minutes. Meanwhile, combine the flour and baking powder in a bowl, then gently whisk in the ale until smooth, thick and coating the back of a spoon nicely. Place a medium, deep pan over a high heat, pour in the sunflower or sunseed oil and allow to heat up. To test if the oil is hot enough, drop a piece of bread into the pan – if it floats to the surface, sizzles and turns golden, it's about right. Drain the onions, dust a handful of them with flour until lightly coated, then dip them into the batter. Remove with a slotted spoon and allow any excess batter to drip off, then carefully lower into the hot oil. Cook for around 1 minute, or until golden and crisp, turning halfway with the slotted spoon. Transfer to a double layer of kitchen paper to drain, then repeat with the remaining onion.

CALORIES	FAT	SAT FAT	PROTEIN	CARBS	SUGAR	SALT	FIBRE
249kcal	13.4g	1.7g	3.3g	28g	4.7g	0.5g	1.9g

Liv Tyler's
PRAWN
DUMPLINGS

WATER CHESTNUTS, GINGER & SPRING ONIONS

• • • • • • • • • • • SERVES 6 | TOTAL TIME - 1 HOUR 30 MINUTES • • • • • • • • • • •

Liv's kids are obsessed with Asian food, especially dumplings. With that in mind, I wanted to give her a fail-safe recipe to cook up at home for everyone to enjoy. You can get ahead by making the dumplings in advance, ready to cook to order when you want to tuck in – get your lucky guests ready and waiting at the table.

LIV TYLER'S PRAWN DUMPLINGS
WATER CHESTNUTS, GINGER & SPRING ONIONS

300g raw peeled king or
   tiger prawns, deveined

1 x 140g tin of water
   chestnuts

5cm piece of ginger

6 spring onions

1 large egg

¼ teaspoon ground
   white pepper

1 teaspoon Shaoxing
   rice wine

1 teaspoon sesame oil

vegetable oil

DOUGH

250g dumpling or Tipo 00
   flour, plus extra for
   dusting and cooking

CONDIMENTS

black rice vinegar

chilli oil

sweet chilli sauce

low-salt soy sauce

For the dough, place the flour in a mixing bowl, gradually add 120ml of warm water and bring together into a ball of dough. Knead on a clean flour-dusted surface for 5 minutes, or until smooth, then wrap in clingfilm and leave aside to rest for 30 minutes while you make the filling. Chop two-thirds of the prawns into 1cm cubes, finely chop the rest, then place in a bowl. Drain the water chestnuts, peel the ginger, then finely chop both. Trim and finely slice the spring onions. Add it all to the bowl, then beat and add the egg, along with a good pinch of sea salt, the white pepper, Shaoxing rice wine and sesame oil. Mix well.

On a clean flour-dusted surface, knead the dough a few times, then cut in half. Cover half the dough with a clean damp tea towel while you roll the rest into a sausage, roughly 40cm long. Break off 1.5cm pieces and roll each one into a ball, then flatten into an 8cm round, roughly 2mm thick. Using a pastry brush, lightly brush around the edge of each round with water, then dot 1 level tablespoon of filling in the centre. Fold the dough in half over the filling, cupping your hands around to seal and get rid of any air bubbles. Make the edge wavy like a shell, placing the dumplings on a floured plate as you go.

To cook the dumplings, put a large non-stick frying pan on a medium heat with 1 tablespoon of vegetable oil. Arrange the first batch of dumplings inside and fry until golden on the bottom. Meanwhile, whisk 4 heaped teaspoons of flour with 800ml of water (re-whisk between batches). Once the dumpling bottoms are golden, pour in enough floury water to come 1cm up the side of the pan. Cover with a tight-fitting lid and simmer for 5 minutes, then remove the lid until it begins to fry again – you'll notice a delicate pancake starting to form and encase the dumplings. When it's nicely golden, confidently bang it out upside down on to a serving board. Repeat with the remaining dumplings and floury water. Mix up your own dipping sauce, to taste, using a combination of the condiments. Delicious served as part of a wider dim sum selection.

CALORIES	FAT	SAT FAT	PROTEIN	CARBS	SUGAR	SALT	FIBRE
230kcal	4.6g	0.7g	16.4g	30.9g	2.1g	0.7g	1.1g

ULTIMATE ROAST CHICKEN CAESAR SALAD

PEPPERCORN, FENNEL, APPLE & CHILLI BRINE

• • • • • • SERVES 10-12 | TOTAL TIME - 2 HOURS 15 MINUTES, PLUS BRINING • • • • • •

Take your chicken Caesar salad to the absolute next level by brining the chicken overnight in fresh apple juice, herbs and spices, adding loads of flavour, juiciness and caramelization. Roasting the croutons in the chicken juices creates the ultimate texture plus out-of-this-world tastiness. You've got to try this!

ULTIMATE ROAST CHICKEN CAESAR SALAD
PEPPERCORN, FENNEL, APPLE & CHILLI BRINE

1 x 2.5kg whole chicken

400g sourdough bread

1 bulb of garlic

olive oil

1 x 50g tin of anchovies in oil

1 bunch of fresh
  flat-leaf parsley (30g)

2 fresh red chillies

extra virgin olive oil

1 lemon

4 romaine lettuces

150g mixed-colour radishes

1 cucumber

½ a bunch of fresh chives (15g)

BRINE

4 tablespoons black peppercorns

4 tablespoons fennel seeds

2 litres fresh apple juice

100g sea salt

½ a bunch of fresh thyme (15g)

12 fresh bay leaves

6 dried red chillies

CAESAR DRESSING

50g Parmesan cheese,
  plus extra to serve

1 teaspoon English mustard

2 teaspoons Worcestershire sauce

250g Greek yoghurt

1 lemon

For the brine, toast the peppercorns and fennel seeds in a large pot over a high heat for 1 minute, then add the apple juice, sea salt, thyme and bay leaves. Crumble in the dried chillies and bring to the boil, then turn the heat off, top up with 1 litre of cold water and leave to cool. Use a sharp knife to carefully cut down the back of the chicken so you can open it out flat, then add to the cooled brine (transfer to a bigger container, if needed). Cover and refrigerate for at least 12 hours, then drain and pat dry with kitchen paper.

Preheat the oven to 200°C/400°F/gas 6. Roughly tear the sourdough into big chunks, break up the garlic bulb, and put aside. Rub 1 tablespoon of olive oil all over the chicken and place it directly on the bars of the oven, skin side up, with a large tray underneath to catch the juices. Roast for 30 minutes, then reduce the temperature to 160°C/325°F/gas 3. Add the sourdough and unpeeled garlic cloves to the tray and carefully toss to coat in the juices. Roast for 1 hour, or until the chicken is golden and cooked through, tossing the croutons occasionally. Leave the chicken to rest for 30 minutes before carving. Meanwhile, drain the anchovies (saving the oil) and

halve lengthways, then arrange on a plate in a criss-cross fashion. Finely chop the parsley stalks (reserving the leaves), finely slice or chop the chillies, and scatter both over the anchovies. Drizzle over ½ a tablespoon each of the reserved anchovy oil and extra virgin olive oil, then finely grate over half the lemon zest and squeeze over half the juice. Leave to marinate. For the Caesar dressing, finely grate the Parmesan into a bowl, add the mustard, Worcestershire sauce and yoghurt, and whisk to combine. Squeeze in the lemon juice, add 8 tablespoons of extra virgin olive oil and mix again. Taste and season to perfection, loosening with a splash of water, if needed. Trim the lettuces and radishes and scrape a fork down the sides of the cucumber. Finely slice the radishes, cucumber, parsley leaves and chives, roughly chop the lettuces, and place everything in a large bowl.

Add half the croutons to the salad, pour over half the dressing and toss together, then use a speed-peeler to shave over a little Parmesan. Arrange the chicken and remaining croutons on a board, then serve it all up with the anchovies and extra dressing. Let everyone dig in.

CALORIES	FAT	SAT FAT	PROTEIN	CARBS	SUGAR	SALT	FIBRE
502kcal	27.5g	7.7g	38.1g	25.9g	5.2g	2.1g	1.6g

Sienna Miller's
DUCK RAGÙ

PICI PASTA & DUCK SKIN PANGRATTATO

· · · · · · · · · · SERVES 8 | TOTAL TIME - 4 HOURS 10 MINUTES · · · · · · · · · ·

Sienna told me about an amazing ragù she'd enjoyed in the Val d'Orcia region of Tuscany, and this is my take on that recipe for her. Think of it as a richer and meatier version of your average Bolognese – it's a real treat, and when topped with amazing duck skin breadcrumbs, it really is out of this world.

SIENNA MILLER'S DUCK RAGÙ
PICI PASTA & DUCK SKIN PANGRATTATO

1 x 2kg whole duck

olive oil

2 medium red onions

4 cloves of garlic

1 stick of celery

300ml Chianti, or other
  red wine

2 x 400g tins of quality
  plum tomatoes

100g raisins

2 sprigs of fresh rosemary

3 fresh bay leaves

1 x Royal pasta dough
  (see page 244)

fine semolina, for dusting

extra virgin olive oil

Parmesan cheese,
  for grating

DUCK SKIN PANGRATTATO

1 clove of garlic

1 thick slice of quality
  stale bread

4 sprigs of fresh thyme

Get the duck out of the fridge and up to room temperature before you cook it. Preheat the oven to 180°C/350°F/gas 4. Rub the duck all over with olive oil, sea salt and black pepper. Put into a snug-fitting roasting tray and roast for 2 hours, or until golden and cooked through, then remove the duck to a board and set the tray aside for later.

Peel the onions, garlic and celery, then finely chop and place in a large, wide pan on a medium-low heat with 1 tablespoon of olive oil. Cook for 10 to 15 minutes, or until softened and lightly golden, stirring occasionally. Meanwhile, remove the duck skin and keep to one side (wear clean rubber gloves!), then shred the meat off the bones. Pour most of the Chianti into the pan and let it reduce for 10 to 15 minutes, then stir in the shredded duck meat. Stir the remaining splash of wine into the roasting tray and scrape all the lovely, crispy bits from the bottom, then pour into the pan. Scrunch in the tomatoes through your clean hands, then add 2 tins' worth of water. Stir in the raisins, strip in the rosemary leaves and add the bay leaves, then simmer for 1 hour 30 minutes, or until thickened and reduced – if you've got any Parmesan rind, throw that in too for an added flavour dimension (just remember to take it out before serving!).

Meanwhile, peel the garlic and place in a food processor with the reserved duck skin. Tear in the bread, strip in the thyme leaves, then blitz until fine. Tip into a frying pan on a medium heat with ½ a tablespoon of olive oil and fry for 3 to 5 minutes, or until golden and crisp, stirring regularly. Decant into a small bowl. Make the royal pasta dough (see page 244). Once it's relaxed for 30 minutes, roll out on a clean flour-dusted surface into a rectangle roughly ½cm thick. Using a sharp knife, cut it into long ½cm strips, then with lightly oiled fingers gently roll each strip into a long thin sausage shape, starting at the middle and carefully rolling outwards, placing them on a semolina-dusted tray as you go.

When the ragù has around 10 minutes to go, cook the pici in a large pan of boiling salted water for 6 to 10 minutes, or until al dente. Drain, reserving a cupful of cooking water. Toss the pici with the ragù, adding a splash of extra virgin olive oil and a little reserved cooking water to loosen, if needed. Divide between bowls, then grate over some Parmesan, sprinkle over the pangrattato, and serve.

CALORIES	FAT	SAT FAT	PROTEIN	CARBS	SUGAR	SALT	FIBRE
809kcal	47.8g	12.4g	30.3g	60g	14.9g	0.4g	3.4g

Tom Daley's
SWEET & SOUR
CHICKEN

TEAMED WITH A RAINBOW OF VEG

· · · · · · · · · · · · · SERVES 4 | TOTAL TIME - 35 MINUTES · · · · · · · · · · · · ·

Tom told me this is his guilty pleasure after a competition, so I wanted to show him just how fantastic it can be if you make it from scratch. The joy of cooking at home is that you can really own it – packed with fresh veg, and free from piles of added sugar and fat often found in takeaways, this firm favourite is a real winner.

TOM DALEY'S SWEET & SOUR CHICKEN
TEAMED WITH A RAINBOW OF VEG

1 x 227g tin of pineapple in natural juice

1 x 213g tin of peaches in natural juice

1 tablespoon low-salt soy sauce

1 tablespoon fish sauce

2 teaspoons cornflour

2 x 120g chicken breasts, skin on

Chinese five-spice

1 lime

2 cloves of garlic

1 bunch of asparagus (350g)

100g tenderstem broccoli

1 small onion

2 fresh red chillies

1 red pepper

1 yellow pepper

7cm piece of ginger

groundnut oil

100g baby sweetcorn

1 teaspoon runny honey

½ a bunch of fresh coriander (15g)

Drain the juices from the tinned fruit into a bowl, add the soy and fish sauces, then whisk in 1 teaspoon of cornflour until smooth. Chop the pineapple and peaches into bite-sized chunks and put aside. Pull off the chicken skin, lay it flat in a large, cold frying pan, place on a low heat and leave for a few minutes to render the fat, turning occasionally. Once golden, remove the crispy skin to a plate, adding a pinch of sea salt and five-spice. Meanwhile, slice the chicken into 3cm chunks and place in a bowl with 1 heaped teaspoon of five-spice, a pinch of salt, 1 teaspoon of cornflour and half the lime juice. Peel, finely chop and add 1 clove of garlic, then toss to coat.

Next, prep the veg: trim and roughly slice the asparagus and broccoli at an angle, leaving the pretty tips intact. Peel the onion, cut into quarters and break apart into petals, then peel the remaining clove of garlic and finely slice with the chillies. Deseed and roughly chop the peppers, then peel and matchstick the ginger. Place the frying pan on a high heat and cook the chicken for 5 to 6 minutes, or until golden and cooked through, turning halfway, then leave on a low heat.

Meanwhile, place a wok on a high heat and scatter in the pepper and onion to scald and char for 5 minutes. Add 1 tablespoon of oil, followed by the peaches, pineapple, ginger, garlic, most of the chillies, the baby sweetcorn, asparagus and broccoli. Stir-fry for 3 minutes, then pour in the sauce. Cook for just a few minutes – you want to keep the veg on the edge of raw – adding a good splash of boiling water to loosen the sauce, if needed.

Drizzle the honey into the chicken pan, turn the heat back up to high, and toss until sticky and caramelized. Plate up the veg and top with the chicken. Clank up the reserved crispy skin, and scatter over with the remaining chilli. Pick over the coriander leaves and serve right away, with lime wedges for squeezing over. Good with classic fluffy rice.

CALORIES	FAT	SAT FAT	PROTEIN	CARBS	SUGAR	SALT	FIBRE
278kcal	9.4g	2.2g	22.4g	27.6g	22.1g	1.6g	3.5g

Kate Hudson's
HOT & SMOKY
VINDALOO

PUNCHY PORK BELLY WITH FRAGRANT SPICES

· · · · · · · · · · · · SERVES 6 | TOTAL TIME – 1 HOUR 40 MINUTES · · · · · · · · · · · ·

I rustled up this proper vindaloo for Kate, who's always loved her mum's home-cooked version. With soft pork belly, sweet caramelized onions and a gorgeous gravy, this Goan curry is spicy, sour and a little bit sweet – it's all about rich and subtle flavours, not blow-your-head-off heat! Trust me, you'll love it.

KATE HUDSON'S HOT & SMOKY VINDALOO
PUNCHY PORK BELLY WITH FRAGRANT SPICES

. . . .

2 heaped teaspoons
    coriander seeds

1 teaspoon cumin seeds

1 heaped teaspoon
    black peppercorns

2 dried Kashmiri chillies

5cm piece of ginger

6 cloves of garlic

1 teaspoon ground
    turmeric

olive oil

1 tablespoon cider vinegar

1kg pork belly,
    skin removed

3 small onions

1 handful of curry
    leaves

2 fresh mixed-colour
    chillies

1 tablespoon
    tamarind paste

1 heaped tablespoon
    soft brown sugar

1 stick of cinnamon

4 cloves

You also need:
1 piece of charcoal

Preheat the oven to 170°C/325°F/gas 3. Place a large, wide, ovenproof pan on a medium-high heat with the coriander and cumin seeds and the peppercorns. Crumble in the dried chillies and toast it all for 1 minute, or until smelling fantastic. Tip into a pestle and mortar and bash to a fine powder. Peel and roughly chop the ginger and garlic, pound into the mortar with the turmeric, then muddle in 1 tablespoon of oil and the vinegar.

Using a sharp knife, chop the pork belly into rough 2cm chunks. Return the pan to a medium-high heat with the pork and season with a little sea salt. Fry for 15 minutes, or until golden all over. Meanwhile, peel and finely slice the onions. Once the pork is golden, add the curry leaves and three-quarters of the curry paste to the pan (save the rest for another day). Toss well, then add the onions and cook for a further 15 minutes, or until golden, stirring occasionally. Finely chop the fresh chillies, then stir into the pan with the tamarind paste and sugar. Transfer to the oven for around 25 minutes, or until darkened.

Take the pan out of the oven and skim away any excess fat (store in an airtight jar in the fridge for epic roasties another day). Place the pan on a high heat, add 600ml of boiling water and bring to the boil, then reduce to a simmer. Place the charcoal and cinnamon stick over a direct flame on the hob, turning with tongs until the charcoal starts to smoke and turn white. Place both in a small heatproof bowl with the cloves, then sit the bowl directly in the middle of the vindaloo pan (like you see in the picture on the previous page). Drizzle over a drop of oil until the charcoal starts to smoke like incense. Carefully cover the pan with a double layer of tin foil and poke a hole in the top to allow the smoke to escape. Put the curry back in the oven and cook for around 20 minutes, or until the meat is tender; or, if you prefer it falling apart, cook it for 1 hour longer, topping up with water if it gets too dry. Remove the charcoal bowl before serving. I like to dish up with homemade naan breads, a simple baby gem salad and raita.

CALORIES	FAT	SAT FAT	PROTEIN	CARBS	SUGAR	SALT	FIBRE
751kcal	59g	19.8g	43.8g	95.7g	13g	2.5g	3g

Michael McIntyre's
SCALLOPS FOR KITTY
CRISPY PANCETTA, ANCHOVIES, BROCCOLI & BEANS

••••••••••••• SERVES 2 | TOTAL TIME - 20 MINUTES •••••••••••••

Michael and his wife, Kitty, enjoyed scallops just like this on one of their first dates. They were at the River Café, where I used to work back in the day, so it was a real treat for me to reminisce and recreate that vibe for them here. Make this special dish for someone you love and really knock their socks off!

MICHAEL MCINTYRE'S SCALLOPS FOR KITTY
CRISPY PANCETTA, ANCHOVIES, BROCCOLI & BEANS

1½ cloves of garlic

½ a fresh red chilli

olive oil

2 sprigs of fresh rosemary

1 x 400g tin of borlotti
beans

1 teaspoon red or
white wine vinegar

150g tenderstem broccoli

2 anchovy fillets in oil

extra virgin olive oil

½ a lemon

6 scallops, trimmed,
roes attached

4 thin rashers of smoked
pancetta

2 sprigs of fresh sage

Peel and finely slice 1 clove of garlic, deseed and finely chop the chilli, then place in a frying pan on a medium heat with 1 tablespoon of olive oil. Strip the leaves off 1 sprig of rosemary, finely chop, add to the pan and cook for 1 minute. Tip in the beans (juice and all) to warm through, then add the vinegar and season with sea salt and black pepper. Leave to tick away, adding splashes of water, if needed.

Trim the broccoli, halving any thicker stems lengthways, cook in a pan of boiling salted water for 6 minutes, or until just tender, then drain. Meanwhile, strip the remaining rosemary into a pestle and mortar, peel and add the remaining ½ clove of garlic along with the anchovies, pound well, then muddle in 2 tablespoons of extra virgin olive oil (or use oil from the anchovy tin) and a squeeze of lemon juice.

Season the scallops with a pinch of salt. Place a frying pan on a high heat with 1 tablespoon of olive oil, and cook the scallops and pancetta for 1 to 1½ minutes on each side, depending on the size of the scallops. Pick in the sage leaves for the last minute, add a squeeze of lemon juice and toss together, then remove from the heat.

Toss the drained broccoli with a drizzle of the anchovy dressing, to taste (save the rest for another day). Spoon the beans on to a serving plate and top with the dressed broccoli, then the scallops, crispy pancetta and sage.

I've used tinned beans here for ease, but when they're in season, look out for fresh borlotti beans at your local market. Pod and cook in a pan of boiling water with one whole peeled potato, a handful of cherry tomatoes and a few sprigs of fresh thyme and bay for 45 minutes, or until softened. Add good extra virgin olive oil and vinegar, season to perfection, and you're good to go!

CALORIES	FAT	SAT FAT	PROTEIN	CARBS	SUGAR	SALT	FIBRE
459kcal	30.1g	5.1g	28.1g	19.2g	2.7g	1.5g	10.2g

MEGA MEATBALL SUB

LOADED WITH CHEESE & LASHINGS OF GRAVY

This gorgeous comfort food dish is super-easy to put together and delivers big on the flavour front. You end up with a mega tray of oozy cheese-topped meatballs in thick, delicious gravy, ready to be spooned into warm subs. The best bit? There'll be enough of that amazing gravy left for some epic dunking as you tuck in.

olive oil

1 small potato

500g minced pork shoulder

500g minced beef

4 sprigs of fresh rosemary

6 submarine rolls

red wine vinegar

100g Red Leicester cheese

50g watercress

GRAVY

2 red onions

1 bulb of fennel

1 heaped tablespoon
  plain flour

100ml porter or stout

1 litre quality chicken stock

1 tablespoon HP sauce

1 tablespoon tomato
  ketchup

1 tablespoon
  Worcestershire sauce

1 teaspoon English mustard

1 tablespoon mango
  chutney

Preheat the oven to 200°C/400°F/gas 6. Lightly oil a large roasting tray. Peel and coarsely grate the potato, then place in a bowl with the minced pork and beef. Scrunch together, then use wet hands to divide and roll the mixture into 21 balls, each slightly larger than a golf ball. Reserving 3, place the rest in the prepared roasting tray and set aside.

To make the gravy, peel the onions, trim the fennel, then finely chop both and place in a large pan on a medium heat with 1 tablespoon of oil. Cook for 10 minutes, or until softened, stirring occasionally. Break in the 3 reserved meatballs, then cook for a further 10 minutes on a high heat, or until dark golden. Stir in the flour for 2 minutes, then add the porter and leave to cook away. Pour in the stock, stir in the remaining gravy ingredients, then bring to the boil. Reduce to a simmer for 20 minutes, or until thick and glossy.

Meanwhile, season the tray of meatballs with sea salt and black pepper, then cook in the oven for 20 to 25 minutes, or until golden and cooked through. Transfer the tray to a medium heat on the hob, pour over the gravy, add the rosemary sprigs and simmer for a few minutes while you warm the rolls in the cooling oven. Stir a splash of vinegar into the gravy, then grate over the cheese and turn off the heat. Slice open the rolls, then spoon in the cheesy meatballs and gravy. Top with pinches of watercress, and serve with any leftover gravy for dunking. Epic!

CALORIES	FAT	SAT FAT	PROTEIN	CARBS	SUGAR	SALT	FIBRE
691kcal	32.6g	14.2g	49.7g	46.7g	10.2g	2.3g	4.4g

BEAUTIFUL VEGGIE MOUSSAKA

GOLDEN AUBERGINES, SOFT POTATOES & VEG RAGÙ

• • • • • • • • • • • SERVES 12 | TOTAL TIME - 2 HOURS 30 MINUTES • • • • • • • • • •

Traditional moussaka is made with lamb, but I've rustled up an epic veggie version that everyone can enjoy. Using dried porcini mushrooms gives an amazingly robust flavour to the ragù, and the lentils and chickpeas will make sure this dish satisfies even the heartiest appetite. It's rich, it's creamy, it's delicious – you're gonna love it!

BEAUTIFUL VEGGIE MOUSSAKA
GOLDEN AUBERGINES, SOFT POTATOES & VEG RAGÙ

15g dried porcini
   mushrooms

2 onions

2 cloves of garlic

olive oil

4 sprigs of fresh rosemary

4 sprigs of fresh sage

dried oregano

250ml red wine

1 x 660g jar of chickpeas

100g dried brown lentils

4 fresh bay leaves

2 x 400g tins of quality
   plum tomatoes

4 large firm aubergines

800g potatoes

750ml semi-skimmed milk

5 black peppercorns

75g unsalted butter

75g plain flour

50g feta cheese

50g kefalotyri or
   pecorino cheese

2 large eggs

Preheat the oven to 180°C/350°F/gas 4. Just cover the porcini with boiling water, then set aside to rehydrate. Peel and finely slice the onions and garlic, then place in a large pan over a medium-low heat with 1 tablespoon of oil. Strip in the rosemary and sage leaves and add 1 teaspoon of dried oregano. Roughly chop the porcini (reserving the soaking liquor) and add to the pan, then fry for 10 minutes, or until softened, stirring occasionally. Turn the heat up to high, then add the wine and let it bubble and cook away. Stir in the chickpeas (juice and all), lentils and 2 bay leaves. Scrunch in the tomatoes through your clean hands, then pour in the porcini soaking liquor (discarding just the last gritty bit). Season with sea salt and black pepper, bring to the boil, then simmer on a low heat for 1 hour, or until thickened and reduced, stirring occasionally.

Trim the aubergines and peel with a speed-peeler, leaving a little of the skin to create a stripy effect, then slice into 1cm-thick rounds. Place in a colander, sprinkle with a good pinch of salt and leave in the sink to drain (the salt will draw out the moisture). Peel the potatoes and slice into rough 1cm rounds, then parboil in a pan of boiling salted water for 5 minutes. Drain and leave to steam dry, then place in a large, deep roasting tray (30cm x 40cm). Season, drizzle with oil and scatter over 1 heaped tablespoon of dried oregano. Toss well to coat, then roast in a single layer for 30 to 40 minutes, or until golden and tender. Meanwhile, rinse the aubergines and pat dry with kitchen paper, then spread out across a few large roasting trays. Drizzle with oil, season with pepper and oregano, then roast alongside the potatoes for 30 to 40 minutes, or until golden and cooked through.

Warm the milk with the remaining 2 bay leaves and the peppercorns in a pan on a medium-low heat – keep an eye on it. Before it boils, strain into a jug, then wipe out the pan and return to a medium heat. Melt the butter, then stir in the flour to form a paste. Start adding the hot milk, a splash at a time, stirring in each addition before adding more, until you have a smooth, creamy sauce. Crumble in one-third of the feta and grate in one-third of the kefalotyri, then simmer over a low heat for a further 5 minutes, or until thick and smooth. Leave to cool slightly.

To assemble, spoon half the ragù over the tray of potatoes, then layer half the aubergines on top. Repeat with the remaining ragù and aubergines. Separate the eggs (saving the whites for another recipe). Whisk the yolks into the sauce, then pour over the aubergines. Crumble and grate over the remaining cheese, drizzle with oil, and bake for 40 minutes, or until golden. Leave to stand for 30 minutes, then serve. Great with a Greek salad.

CALORIES	FAT	SAT FAT	PROTEIN	CARBS	SUGAR	SALT	FIBRE
311kcal	12.6g	6g	12.6g	35.4g	8.8g	1g	5.8g

SPICED LAMB FLATBREADS

CABBAGE PICKLE, POMEGRANATE & HARISSA

• • • • • • • • • • • SERVES 8 | TOTAL TIME – 7 HOURS 20 MINUTES • • • • • • • • • • •

Gorgeous sticky tomatoes and zingy pickle add a wonderful brightness to this dish, but the super-tender, melt-in-your-mouth lamb is the real star of the show. Delicately spiced and cooked so slowly it falls right off the bone, then shredded into homemade flatbreads, this one's definitely a winner.

SPICED LAMB FLATBREADS
CABBAGE PICKLE, POMEGRANATE & HARISSA

1.4kg lamb shoulder,
  bone in

1 teaspoon cumin seeds

2 teaspoons coriander seeds

1 teaspoon fennel seeds

1 pinch of saffron

white pepper

1 sprig of fresh rosemary

½ a bunch of fresh thyme (15g)

1 orange

100g unsalted butter
  (at room temperature)

1.5kg large ripe tomatoes,
  on the vine

1 bulb of garlic

olive oil

200g plain wholemeal flour,
  plus extra for dusting

2 cos lettuce

1 pomegranate

2 tablespoons rose harissa

½ a bunch of fresh mint (15g)

150ml Greek yoghurt

1 tablespoon red wine vinegar

CABBAGE PICKLE

½ a red cabbage (400g)

½ a bunch of fresh
  flat-leaf parsley (15g)

2 tablespoons red wine vinegar

1 pinch of ground cloves

Preheat the oven to full whack (240°C/475°F/gas 9). Using a sharp knife, score a criss-cross pattern into any fat on the lamb shoulder. Pound the cumin, coriander and fennel seeds, the saffron and a good pinch of sea salt and white pepper in a pestle and mortar. Strip in the rosemary leaves and 2 thyme sprigs, finely grate in the orange zest, then muddle in the softened butter until combined. Rub all over the lamb, then tightly wrap in a layer of damp greaseproof paper and tin foil. Put into a roasting tray and place on the top shelf of the oven. Immediately reduce the temperature to 130°C/250°F/gas ½, and cook for 7 hours, or until falling off the bone.

Halve the tomatoes and place in a large roasting tray with the bulb of garlic. Strip in the remaining thyme leaves, drizzle with oil and season with salt and black pepper. Place in the oven, underneath the lamb, for the last 4 hours, so the tomatoes are super-soft and caramelized.

To make the pickle, finely slice the cabbage, then roughly chop the top leafy half of the parsley. Place in a large bowl and mix well with the vinegar and cloves. For the flatbreads, mix the flour, a good pinch of salt and 120ml of cold water into a dough. Knead on a clean flour-dusted surface for 2 minutes, then divide into 8 balls. Roll each into a thin round. In batches, cook the flatbreads in a large non-stick frying pan for 1 minute on each side, or until cooked but not coloured. Keep warm, wrapped in foil as you go. Shred the lettuce, then halve the pomegranate and, holding one half cut side down in your fingers, gently bash it with the back of a wooden spoon so all the seeds tumble out, and repeat.

Decant the harissa into a bowl and season to perfection. Pick the mint leaves, pound in a pestle and mortar, then mix with the yoghurt and vinegar.

Once ready, remove the tomatoes from the oven, squeeze the soft garlic out of their skins and mix. Using two forks, shred the lamb, removing and discarding the bones and any wobbly bits. Serve everything in the middle of the table and let everyone build their own delicious flatbread.

CALORIES	FAT	SAT FAT	PROTEIN	CARBS	SUGAR	SALT	FIBRE
416kcal	22.9g	10.3g	26.7g	28.2g	11.1g	1g	6.9g

GAME-ON CURRY

CHICKEN, QUAIL, PARTRIDGE, PHEASANT & AUBERGINES

• • • • • • • • • • • • SERVES 8 | TOTAL TIME – 1 HOUR 20 MINUTES • • • • • • • • • • • •

There are so many beautiful game birds you can cook with these days. Plus, game is seasonal, so it's often better value than supermarket birds. If you're nervous, ease yourself in gently by upping the ratio of chicken. Trust me, it's delicious!

GAME-ON CURRY

CHICKEN, QUAIL, PARTRIDGE, PHEASANT & AUBERGINES

. . . .

2 x 200g chicken legs

1 quail

1 partridge

1 pheasant

1 big handful of curry
leaves

8 finger aubergines

8 small round aubergines

1 large aubergine (400g)

1 x 400g tin of light
coconut milk

PASTE

1 onion

4 cloves of garlic

4cm piece of ginger

2 fresh red chillies

1 bunch of fresh
coriander (30g)

4 teaspoons crunchy
peanut butter

4 teaspoons tamarind paste

2 heaped teaspoons soft
brown sugar

2 teaspoons each
fenugreek seeds,
garam masala

1 teaspoon each cumin
seeds, fennel seeds,
ground turmeric

Preheat the oven to 190°C/375°F/gas 5. For the paste, peel the onion, garlic and ginger, deseed the chillies, then slice it all with the coriander stalks (reserving the leaves). Place it all in a large ovenproof pan on a medium heat and char for 1 to 2 minutes to soften slightly. Tip into a large pestle and mortar, add the remaining paste ingredients and bash to a thick paste (or whiz in a food processor).

Return the pan to a medium heat. Halve the chicken legs through the bone, then place skin side down in the pan with the quail. Cut off and add the partridge and pheasant legs. Remove and discard the partridge and pheasant backbones, then halve the birds and add to the pan. Dry-fry for 3 to 4 minutes, or until everything is golden all over, then add the curry leaves and 1 heaped tablespoon of the paste. Leave to tick away on a low heat while you prep the aubergines, stirring regularly.

Leaving the finger and round aubergines intact at the stalk, cut into quarters lengthways. Cut the large aubergine into thick rounds and slice down into the outer edge of each round to make a pocket. Use the remaining paste to stuff all the aubergines and coat their outsides. Layer into the pan on top of the game – it'll be snug! Transfer to the oven to cook for 40 minutes, or until the aubergines are tender and the meat is cooked through.

Put the pan back on a medium heat on the hob, then pour in the coconut milk and a splash of water. Let it gently bubble away for 2 minutes, then season to perfection with sea salt and black pepper and sprinkle over the coriander leaves. Delicious served with pickles, salad, rice and Fluffy coconut breads (see page 119).

CALORIES	FAT	SAT FAT	PROTEIN	CARBS	SUGAR	SALT	FIBRE
329kcal	15g	5.7g	37.6g	12.3g	8.6g	0.4g	1.2g

FLUFFY COCONUT BREADS

················· MAKES 8 | TOTAL TIME – 15 MINUTES ·················

With minimal ingredients, this recipe couldn't be easier, and the results are unreal. Puffed up and fluffy once cooked, they act like little sponges to mop up curry sauce. Simply brilliant!

1 x 400g tin of light
   coconut milk

450g self-raising flour,
   plus extra for dusting

olive oil

30g unsalted butter

Pour the coconut milk into a bowl with a pinch of sea salt and add enough flour to create a dough (you might not need it all), bringing it together with your hands. On a clean flour-dusted surface, divide into 8 balls, then flatten each into a 10cm round, pushing your fingers into the top to give you a ripple effect. Place on a lightly oiled tray, and cover with a clean damp tea towel until you're ready to cook. Working in batches, drizzle a little oil into a large non-stick frying pan on a medium heat with some of the butter. Once melted, cook a few dough rounds for 2 to 3 minutes on each side, or until golden and puffed up, then repeat. Delicious served with my Game-on curry (see page 118).

CALORIES	FAT	SAT FAT	PROTEIN	CARBS	SUGAR	SALT	FIBRE
259kcal	7.9g	4.8g	5.5g	44g	2g	0.8g	2g

THE ULTIMATE STEAK & ROASTIES

HOMEMADE FLAVOURED VINEGAR

With this recipe I want to show you how to cook a really luxurious cut of beef in the perfect way. And to go with it, I've given you the most mind-blowing roast potatoes you'll ever taste – I squash the spuds to get extra surface area for crispiness, then spritz them with a homemade flavoured vinegar for an amazing added hit of flavour.

1kg French-trimmed côte de boeuf, with a good layer of intramuscular fat

1.8kg Maris Piper potatoes

1 bulb of garlic

olive oil

1 knob of unsalted butter

2 sprigs of fresh rosemary

½ a bunch of fresh woody herbs (15g), such as thyme, oregano, rosemary

extra virgin olive oil

FLAVOURED VINEGAR

2 sprigs of fresh rosemary

50ml cider, white wine or red wine vinegar

½ teaspoon fennel seeds or dried chilli flakes

Get the meat out of the fridge and up to room temperature before you cook it. Preheat the oven to 200°C/400°F/gas 6 and place a large roasting tray inside to heat up. Peel the potatoes, halving any larger ones, then parboil in a pan of boiling salted water for around 12 minutes. Drain, chuff up and leave to steam dry while you separate and bash the unpeeled garlic cloves. Carefully remove the hot tray from the oven and drizzle in 1 tablespoon of olive oil, then add the butter, rosemary sprigs and garlic, followed by the potatoes. Gently toss to coat, then season with sea salt and roast for 45 minutes to 1 hour, or until beautifully golden and crisp.

Meanwhile, put your chosen flavoured vinegar ingredients into a small water spritzer and set aside. Make a herb brush by tying the woody herbs to the end of a wooden spoon with string. Put a large ovenproof frying pan on a high heat to get nice and hot. Drizzle in 1 tablespoon of olive oil, season the steak well and add to the pan, fat side down. Leave for a few minutes so the fat renders out. Now sear for around 8 minutes, or until browned all over, turning and basting with the herb brush every minute or so. Transfer the pan to the oven for 15 minutes for medium, or until cooked to your liking, turning halfway. Move the steak to a board, drizzle with the pan juices and leave to rest.

A few minutes before the roast potatoes are ready, spritz them with the flavoured vinegar – not too much, you want it to be subtle. Return them to the oven for 30 seconds, then lightly squash them with a fish slice. Spritz again and return to the oven for a final few minutes. Slice up the steak and sprinkle with a little salt. Mix a splash of extra virgin olive oil into the resting juices, then drizzle over the steak. Serve with the vinegary roasties. I like to have a good pinch of watercress and a dollop of mustard on the side, too.

CALORIES	FAT	SAT FAT	PROTEIN	CARBS	SUGAR	SALT	FIBRE
730kcal	41.4g	17.2g	38.2g	54.1g	2.2g	1.3g	4.2g

Sarah Millican's
TUSCAN SAUSAGE & TOMATO PASTA

FENNEL, CHILLI, OREGANO & BASIL

· · · · · · · · · · · · · · SERVES 4 | TOTAL TIME – 50 MINUTES · · · · · · · · · · · · · ·

Using best-quality sausages and tomatoes gives this from-scratch version of Sarah's favourite comfort food a real smack of flavour. Finish with freshly grated Parmesan and fresh basil, and it's a real step up from the microwave meals Sarah's used to.

SARAH MILLICAN'S TUSCAN SAUSAGE & TOMATO PASTA
FENNEL, CHILLI, OREGANO & BASIL

1 onion

1 carrot

1 stick of celery

1 bunch of fresh basil (30g)

olive oil

4 quality Italian sausages
(250g in total)

1 heaped teaspoon fennel
seeds

1 teaspoon dried oregano,
ideally the flowering kind

1 pinch of dried chilli flakes

1 sprig of fresh rosemary

4 cloves of garlic

2 tablespoons balsamic
vinegar

2 x 400g tins of quality
plum tomatoes

300g dried penne

40g Parmesan cheese,
plus extra to serve

extra virgin olive oil

Peel the onion, carrot and celery, then finely chop with the basil stalks (reserving the leaves). Place a large pan on a medium-high heat with 2 tablespoons of olive oil, then squeeze the sausagemeat out of the skins into the pan, breaking it up with a wooden spoon as you go. Fry for a few minutes, then add the fennel seeds, oregano and chilli flakes, and strip in the rosemary. Stir in the chopped veg and basil stalks, then peel and finely grate in the garlic. Cook for 10 minutes, or until softened, stirring occasionally.

Pour the balsamic into the pan and leave to bubble away and reduce slightly. Scrunch in the tomatoes through your clean hands, then add 1 tin's worth of water and the larger basil leaves. Bring to the boil, then simmer over a low heat for 20 minutes, or until thickened. With around 10 minutes to go, cook the pasta in a pan of boiling salted water according to the packet instructions, then drain, reserving a mugful of cooking water.

Toss the drained pasta into the sausage pan, loosening with a little reserved cooking water, if needed. Taste and season to perfection with sea salt and black pepper, then remove from the heat. Finely grate in the Parmesan, scatter over the remaining basil leaves, and finish with a drizzle of extra virgin olive oil. Delicious served with pinches of lemony rocket and an extra grating of Parmesan.

CALORIES	FAT	SAT FAT	PROTEIN	CARBS	SUGAR	SALT	FIBRE
591kcal	22g	6.9g	26.3g	76.6g	18.2g	0.6g	5.7g

ROASTED SALMON & ARTICHOKES

FRESH HERBS & TOASTED ALMOND CRUMB

SERVES 12-14 | TOTAL TIME - 1 HOUR 25 MINUTES, PLUS RESTING

I want to show you what an incredible showstopper whole sides of salmon can make. So, next time you've got friends coming over, treat them (and yourself) to this wonder – all the beautiful flavours from the stuffing mingle with the fish and smoky bacon to create a taste sensation that you have to eat to believe! A perfect weekend feast.

olive oil

2 x 1kg sides of salmon,
  skin on, scaled, pin-boned

100g blanched almonds

2 cloves of garlic

2 lemons

100g stale ciabatta

2 fresh baby Italian
  artichokes

1 x 280g jar of artichoke
  hearts in oil

1 bunch of fresh mint (30g)

12 rashers of smoked
  streaky bacon

1 bunch of fresh
  thyme (30g)

Preheat the oven to 220°C/425°F/gas 7. Line a large baking tray with greaseproof paper and rub with a little oil. Lay 8 pieces (roughly an arm's length each) of butcher's string at 5cm intervals widthways across the tray, then place one salmon fillet on top, skin side down. Toast the almonds in a dry frying pan until golden, tossing regularly, then tip into a food processor. Peel, roughly chop and add the garlic, finely grate in the lemon zest, then tear in the ciabatta. Season with black pepper, then pulse until finely chopped. Carefully layer the crumbs over the salmon.

Halve 1 lemon. Trim the fresh artichoke stalks 2cm from the base. Peel away the tough outer leaves until you reach the paler ones that are tender enough to eat, then trim the heads to 3cm, rubbing with the cut lemon as you go to prevent discoloration. Halve them, scoop out and discard the hairy chokes, then finely slice. Drain and roughly slice the jarred artichoke hearts, reserving the oil. Drizzle 1 tablespoon of artichoke oil into a large frying pan on a high heat and fry all the artichokes for 2 minutes. Pick and roughly chop the mint leaves, scatter into the pan, then remove from the heat.

Spoon the artichoke mixture evenly over the breadcrumb layer, drizzle with 1 more tablespoon of artichoke oil, then lay the other salmon fillet on top, skin side up. Arrange the bacon on top in a criss-cross pattern, and sprinkle over the thyme sprigs. Tie the string up and around both fillets to secure the filling. Drizzle over a little extra artichoke oil and sprinkle any excess crumbs back over. Place in the middle of the oven and immediately reduce the temperature to 180°C/350°F/gas 4. Roast for 35 to 40 minutes, or until the bacon and salmon skin are golden and crisp. Rest for 10 minutes, then serve with lemon wedges for squeezing over. Delicious with buttered new potatoes and a crisp green salad.

CALORIES	FAT	SAT FAT	PROTEIN	CARBS	SUGAR	SALT	FIBRE
451kcal	30.2g	5g	38.5g	6.2g	0.7g	1.1g	1.3g

Craig David's
GRENADIAN
BAKED CHICKEN

RICE & PEAS, PUMPKIN & SALSA

• • • SERVES 4 | TOTAL TIME – 1 HOUR 50 MINUTES, PLUS SOAKING & MARINATING • • •

This is a deep dive into proper, old-school Grenadian cuisine, in honour of Craig's family – this is exactly the kind of thing that his late grandmother would have been rustling up at home. It takes a bit of time, but that's kind of the point – it's a labour of love, but the results are truly delicious. Give it a go.

CRAIG DAVID'S GRENADIAN BAKED CHICKEN
RICE & PEAS, PUMPKIN & SALSA

3 onions

8 cloves of garlic

5cm piece of ginger

1–2 Scotch bonnet chillies

6 pimento (allspice) seeds

¼ teaspoon ground cloves

1 whole nutmeg, for grating

1 chicken stock cube

1 x 1.4kg whole chicken, cut into 8 pieces (ask your butcher)

1.2kg pumpkin

olive oil

white pepper

RICE & PEAS

200g dried kidney beans

3 cloves of garlic

8 pimento (allspice) seeds

100g creamed coconut

1 green Scotch bonnet chilli

½ a bunch of fresh thyme (15g)

3 spring onions

200g long-grain rice

SAUCE

1 tablespoon dark brown sugar

2 tablespoons apple cider vinegar

1 teaspoon hot pepper sauce

4 tablespoons tomato ketchup

½ a bunch of fresh thyme (15g)

SALSA

½ a cucumber

1 Scotch bonnet chilli

2 fresh bay leaves

2 tablespoons apple cider vinegar

Soak the kidney beans for the rice and peas in 1 litre of water overnight. To make a marinade for the chicken, peel and grate 1 onion, 4 cloves of garlic and the ginger, then finely slice the Scotch bonnets. Bash the pimento seeds in a pestle and mortar until fine, then add the ground cloves, a pinch of black pepper and a few scrapings of nutmeg. Mix in the grated mixture, stock cube and chillies, then rub all over the chicken. Cover, then marinate in the fridge overnight.

The next day, preheat the oven to 180°C/350°F/gas 4. For the rice and peas, peel and smash the garlic, then place in a pan with the pimento seeds, creamed coconut and beans (soaking water and all). Cook on a medium-low heat with the lid on for 1 hour, or until just tender. Place the chicken in a roasting tray and roast for 40 minutes. Meanwhile, mix all the sauce ingredients, except for the thyme, together. When the time's up on the chicken, reduce the temperature to 150°C/300°F/gas 2. Pour the sauce over the chicken, using the thyme to brush it all over, then roast for a further 35 minutes, or until cooked through. Peel

and deseed the pumpkin, then chop into 2cm chunks. Peel and finely chop the remaining 2 onions and 4 cloves of garlic, then place it all in a large pan on a medium-low heat with 1 tablespoon of oil and a few scrapings of nutmeg. Simmer with the lid on for 45 minutes, or until starting to caramelize, adding splashes of water, if needed. Smash half the pumpkin with a fork, then stir back through and season to taste with sea salt and white pepper.

When the kidney beans are tender, prick and add the Scotch bonnet, strip in the thyme leaves, halve the spring onions lengthways and add with the rice. Mix well, just cover with water, then pop the lid on and cook on a medium-high heat for 25 minutes, or until the rice is cooked. For the salsa, randomly chop the cucumber. Finely slice the Scotch bonnet (deseed if you like) and tear over the bay, discarding the stalks. Mix with the vinegar, then season lightly and leave for 20 minutes to lightly pickle. Serve the rice and peas with the chicken, pumpkin and salsa. Finely grate over a little extra nutmeg before serving.

CALORIES	FAT	SAT FAT	PROTEIN	CARBS	SUGAR	SALT	FIBRE
927kcal	33.9g	14g	64.5g	98g	26g	1.7g	6.4g

ASIAN-STYLE SEAFOOD PARCELS

FRAGRANT LEMONGRASS, FRESH GINGER & LIME

SERVES 2 | TOTAL TIME - 45 MINUTES

This mighty recipe is a real celebration of seafood, and for me it ticks every box. The parcels seal in all the amazing Asian flavours, and you're left with a dish that's gorgeously fragrant and seriously satisfying. What a joy!

1 bream fillet, skin on, scaled, pin-boned

2 scallops, trimmed, roes attached

2 large raw shell-on king prawns

75g mussels, scrubbed, debearded

75g clams, scrubbed

½ a stick of lemongrass

1 clove of garlic

2.5cm piece of ginger

2 fresh lime leaves

1 fresh red chilli

4 sprigs of fresh coriander

1 teaspoon fish sauce

½ tablespoon low-salt soy sauce

2 limes

1 bok choi

1 handful of sugar snap peas

50g purple sprouting broccoli

50g choi sum

1 large egg

150g basmati rice

½ tablespoon coconut cream

Preheat the oven to 220°C/425°F/gas 7. Halve the bream fillet and lightly score the skin, then lightly score the scallops in a criss-cross pattern. Peel the prawns, leaving the heads and tails on (for bonus flavour), then run the tip of a knife down their backs and pull out the vein. Put it all into a bowl. Pick through the mussels and clams, discarding any that remain open when tapped. Put aside in a separate bowl.

To make the marinade, trim the lemongrass, peel the garlic and ginger, then roughly chop with the lime leaves, half the chilli (deseed first, if you like) and the coriander stalks (reserving the leaves). Scrape into a pestle and mortar and bash to a smooth paste. Muddle in the fish and soy sauces, squeeze in the juice of 1 lime, then season to perfection with sea salt and black pepper.

Quarter the bok choi, halve the sugar snaps lengthways, trim the broccoli, then slice the choi sum into 5cm chunks. Tear off a 60cm-long piece of wide tin foil and place a slightly smaller piece of greaseproof paper on top. Pile on the greens, add the fish and seafood, then drizzle over the marinade. Beat the egg and brush it around the foil edges, then place another large piece of foil on top. Leaving about 5cm around the filling, fold in the foil to create a sealed parcel. Place on a baking tray, being careful not to pierce the foil, and place the tray on the bottom of the oven for 15 minutes. Meanwhile, put the rice and coconut cream into a medium pan with twice the volume of boiling salted water. Bring to the boil, then cover and cook on a low heat until tender.

Remove the fish parcel from the oven and very carefully cut it open (mind out for the steam!). Place on a platter, discarding any mussels or clams that haven't opened. Finely slice and scatter over the remaining chilli, tear over the coriander leaves, and serve with the rice and lime wedges for squeezing over.

CALORIES	FAT	SAT FAT	PROTEIN	CARBS	SUGAR	SALT	FIBRE
451kcal	7.4g	2.3g	32.3g	68.2g	2.9g	0.9g	2.8g

Scarlett Moffatt's
SCOTCH EGGS
WITH FRESH HERBS & A SPICY KICK

· · · · · · · · · · SERVES 6 | TOTAL TIME - 1 HOUR 10 MINUTES · · · · · · · · · ·

Transform any buffet or picnic into something extra-special with these beauties — golden and perfectly crisp on the outside, juicy and flavour-packed on the inside, plus that all-important runny egg yolk. There are no words. Scarlett told me she likes to dip Scotch eggs in chocolate spread, but I'm not sure I'd endorse that!

SCARLETT MOFFATT'S SCOTCH EGGS
WITH FRESH HERBS & A SPICY KICK

1 sprig of fresh rosemary

1 sprig of fresh sage

600g pork shoulder, diced

1 whole nutmeg, for
  grating

1 pinch of smoked paprika
  or cayenne pepper

3 anchovy fillets in oil

8 large eggs

100g plain flour

200g breadcrumbs

3 litres vegetable oil,
  for frying

Pick the rosemary and sage leaves into a food processor, add the pork shoulder, a good grating of nutmeg, the smoked paprika or cayenne, the anchovies and a pinch of sea salt and black pepper, then blitz to combine. Cook 6 of the eggs in boiling salted water for 5 minutes, then remove to cold water, carefully peeling as soon as cool enough to handle.

Meanwhile, line up three shallow bowls – place the flour in the first, beat the remaining eggs in the second, and tip the breadcrumbs into the third. Divide the meat mixture into six, and roll into balls. Place a ball on the palm of your hand, then pat and flatten until it's big enough to wrap around the egg. Place a peeled egg in the centre and mould the meat up and around it, sealing the egg inside so you end up with a perfectly round ball. Coat it in flour, dunk it in the egg, allowing any excess to drip off, then roll in the breadcrumbs until well coated. Repeat with the remaining ingredients, then chill for 30 minutes.

When you're ready to cook, just under half fill a large sturdy pan with oil – the oil should be 8cm deep, but never fill your pan more than half full – and place on a medium-high heat. Use a thermometer to tell when it's ready (170°C), or add a piece of potato and wait until it turns golden – that's the sign that it's ready to go. Carefully lower one Scotch egg into the pan – after about 8 minutes it should be golden and perfectly cooked through, so scoop it out, drain on kitchen paper and cut it in half to check your timings, then cook the rest, in small batches, adjusting the time, if needed. Delicious served with a dollop of English mustard, a wedge of Westcombe Cheddar, piccalilli, a few salady bits and bobs, and – of course – a nice, cold beer. Happy days!

CALORIES	FAT	SAT FAT	PROTEIN	CARBS	SUGAR	SALT	FIBRE
670kcal	48.4g	10.3g	32.3g	29.4g	1.2g	1.4g	1.2g

WINTER NIGHTS CHILLI
TOPPED WITH APPLE & RED ONION SALSA

When the weather's closing in, it's really great to tuck into a full-flavoured, hearty dish and, for me, a proper, rustic chilli rocks. The meat will fall apart and melt in your mouth. It's moreish and spicy with a clever contrasting salsa.

20g dried porcini
    mushrooms

2 tablespoons fennel seeds

2 tablespoons coriander
    seeds

2 tablespoons smoked
    paprika

1 butternut squash (1.2kg)

olive oil

1kg pork belly, skin off,
    bone out

1kg brisket

2 large onions

150ml balsamic vinegar

2 x 400g tins of cannellini
    beans or chickpeas

2 x 400g tins of quality
    plum tomatoes

4 mixed-colour peppers

2–3 fresh red chillies

1 bunch of fresh
    coriander (30g)

SALSA

1 red onion

2 eating apples

3 tablespoons cider vinegar

3 tablespoons extra
    virgin olive oil

Preheat the oven to 190°C/375°F/gas 5. In a small bowl, just cover the porcini with boiling water and leave to rehydrate. Bash the fennel and coriander seeds, paprika and 1 teaspoon each of sea salt and black pepper in a pestle and mortar. Carefully cut the squash in half lengthways, deseed, then chop into 4cm chunks. Toss with half the spice mixture and a drizzle of olive oil on a baking tray. Roast for 50 minutes, or until golden, then remove from the oven and reduce the temperature to 150°C/300°F/gas 2.

Meanwhile, drizzle both cuts of meat with olive oil and rub with the remaining spice mixture, then place a large casserole pan (at least 30cm wide, 8cm deep) on a medium-high heat. Put the pork and brisket into the pan fat side down and brown on all sides for around 15 minutes in total. Remove both meats to a plate and reduce the heat under the pan to medium. Peel and roughly chop the onions and add to the fat in the pan. Fry for 10 minutes, or until lightly caramelized, stirring regularly. Add the balsamic and the porcini liquor (discarding just the last gritty bit). Roughly chop and add the porcini, followed by the beans (juice and all), then scrunch in the tomatoes through your clean hands. Return both meats to the pan, loosen with a splash of water if needed, then bring to the boil. Season, and sit a layer of wet greaseproof paper directly on the surface. Cover with tin foil and cook in the oven for 5 hours, or until the meat is tender.

Prick the peppers and chillies, then blacken all over in a griddle pan or directly over the flame of a gas hob. Place in a bowl, cover and leave to cool, then peel and deseed them, keeping as much juice as you can for extra flavour. Roughly chop with half the coriander, and toss with a little salt and pepper. When the meat is tender, remove from the oven, break up the meat, then stir in the squash, peppers and chillies. Adjust the consistency with water, if needed, taste and season to perfection, and keep warm.

To finish, make the salsa. Peel the onion, then finely chop with the apples and the remaining coriander. Dress with the cider vinegar and extra virgin olive oil and season to perfection. Serve the chilli with the salsa. Also good with bread or rice, and yoghurt.

CALORIES	FAT	SAT FAT	PROTEIN	CARBS	SUGAR	SALT	FIBRE
553kcal	28.5g	9.5g	40.4g	35.8g	19.9g	0.9g	7.3g

CARBONARA CAKE

SPAGHETTI, SMOKED HAM & LOTSA LOVELY CHEESE

This is a delightfully simple, luxurious, yet slightly trashy meal that is sure to wow everyone. It gives you classic carbonara flavours, but with a crisp exterior to contrast with that creamy interior. Total comfort heaven.

300g dried spaghetti

olive oil

100g hard cheese,
  such as Parmesan,
  Cheddar, Gruyère

3 large eggs

250ml double cream

250g cooked smoked ham

3 sprigs of fresh rosemary

Preheat the oven to 180°C/350°F/gas 4. Cook the spaghetti in a pan of boiling salted water according to the packet instructions, then drain and leave to steam dry and cool in the colander. Meanwhile, rub the inside of a 20cm loose-bottomed cake tin with oil, then finely grate a thin layer of cheese all over the base, shaking it up the sides.

Once the spaghetti is cool, transfer it to a large bowl, gently pulling it apart, then beat and add the eggs, along with the cream and a generous pinch of black pepper. Chop and add the ham, finely grate in the rest of your cheese, and pick, chop and add the rosemary leaves. Toss together well, then pack into the cake tin and place on a baking tray. Bake for 35 minutes, or until golden, crisp and cooked through.

Leave the carbonara cake to sit for 3 minutes in the tin, then carefully and confidently run a knife around the rim and release it proudly on to a board. Great served with a fresh, zingy lemon-dressed salad on the side.

> This is a great base recipe that's able to embrace all sorts of seasonal loveliness at different times of the year – from spring peas and asparagus, to autumn mushrooms or chunks of roasted winter squash.

CALORIES	FAT	SAT FAT	PROTEIN	CARBS	SUGAR	SALT	FIBRE
545kcal	19.1g	10.3g	22.2g	38.4g	2.8g	1.4g	1.9g

Lindsay Lohan's
CHICKEN POT PIE

VEAL MEATBALLS & HOMEMADE PASTRY

· · · · · · · · · · SERVES 8 | TOTAL TIME – 2 HOURS 20 MINUTES · · · · · · · · · ·

Comforting and easy to knock together, this crowd-pleasing chicken pie is jam-packed full of flavour. I've taken it to the next level of deliciousness by sneaking in some fresh sage and veal meatballs, just like the ones Lindsay's grandma used to make. This pie really is something special – you've got to try it.

LINDSAY LOHAN'S CHICKEN POT PIE
VEAL MEATBALLS & HOMEMADE PASTRY

2 onions

2 carrots

2 small potatoes

2 medium leeks

olive oil

300g chicken thighs,
skin off, bone out

300g skinless boneless
chicken breast

4 rashers of smoked
streaky bacon

1 knob of unsalted butter

50g plain flour

700ml quality chicken stock

2 teaspoons English
mustard

1 heaped tablespoon
crème fraîche

½ a bunch of fresh woody
herbs (15g), such as
thyme, bay, rosemary

white pepper

3 sprigs of fresh sage

300g minced veal (20% fat)

1 large egg

PASTRY

300g plain flour, plus extra
for dusting

100g shredded suet

100g unsalted butter (cold)

Preheat the oven to 180°C/350°F/gas 4. Peel and roughly chop the onions and carrots, then peel the potatoes and chop into 2cm chunks. Trim, halve and wash the leeks, then finely slice. Place a large pan on a medium heat with 1 tablespoon of oil. Chop all the chicken into 3cm chunks, roughly chop the bacon, and add both to the pan. Cook for a few minutes, or until lightly golden, stirring occasionally. Add the onions, carrots, potatoes and leeks, then cook for a further 15 minutes, or until softened, stirring occasionally. Add the butter, then stir in the flour to coat. Gradually pour in the stock, stirring continuously, then add the mustard and crème fraîche. Tie the woody herb sprigs together with string to make a bouquet garni and add to the pan. Cook for 10 more minutes, stirring regularly, then season with white pepper.

Meanwhile, for the pastry, put the flour and a good pinch of sea salt into a bowl with the suet, cube and add the butter, then use your thumbs and forefingers to rub the fat into the flour until it resembles coarse breadcrumbs. Slowly stir in 100ml of ice-cold water, then use your hands to gently bring it together into a ball, but don't overwork it. Wrap in clingfilm and place in the fridge to chill for at least 30 minutes, while you make the meatballs. Pick and finely chop the sage, season with salt and pepper, then, using your hands, scrunch and mix with the veal. Roll into 3cm balls, then gently place in a large pan on a medium heat with ½ a tablespoon of oil and cook for 10 minutes, or until golden all over, jiggling occasionally for even cooking.

Transfer the pie filling to a large oval dish (25cm x 30cm), discarding the bouquet garni. Leave to cool, then dot the meatballs on top. Roll out the pastry on a clean flour-dusted surface so it's slightly bigger than your pie dish. Eggwash the edges of the dish, then carefully place the pastry on top of the pie, trimming off any overhang. Pinch the edges to seal, and make a small incision in the centre for the steam to escape. Use any spare pastry to decorate the pie, if you like. Eggwash the top, then bake for around 50 minutes, or until the pastry is golden and the pie is piping hot. Leave to stand for 10 minutes before serving. Really good with steamed seasonal greens.

CALORIES	FAT	SAT FAT	PROTEIN	CARBS	SUGAR	SALT	FIBRE
656kcal	36.3g	18.3g	36.4g	48.9g	6.9g	1.9g	4.6g

FILLET OF BEEF

WRAPPED IN PORCINI & PROSCIUTTO

· SERVES 6 | TOTAL TIME - 1 HOUR 15 MINUTES · · · · · · · · · · · · · · · · · ·

In this wonderfully extravagant showstopper the earthy porcini go hand-in-hand with the garlic, thyme and butter to really kiss the meat as it cooks, creating a flavour-packed meltingly tender treat. Wrapping the fillet in a parcel of prosciutto not only protects it, but also seasons it to perfection as it cooks. Double win!

1kg centre fillet of beef, trimmed

20g dried porcini mushrooms

1 large bulb of garlic

50g unsalted butter

½ a lemon

olive oil

10 large slices of prosciutto or Parma ham

4 sprigs of fresh rosemary

4 sprigs of fresh thyme

250ml red wine

Preheat the oven to 220°C/425°F/gas 7. Get the meat out of the fridge and leave to come up to room temperature before you cook it. Cover the porcini with 300ml of boiling water and leave to rehydrate for 5 minutes. Peel and finely chop 2 of the garlic cloves, then place in a large frying pan on a high heat with a knob of the butter. Add the porcini and half the soaking liquor, then reduce the heat to low and simmer for 5 minutes, or until thick and syrupy. Squeeze in the lemon juice, stir in the remaining butter, and season to taste with sea salt and black pepper. Leave to cool slightly.

Drizzle the beef with 1 tablespoon of oil and season with black pepper. Sear in a sturdy roasting tray over a medium heat on the hob until browned all over, then remove from the heat. Lay out the slices of prosciutto on a large piece of greaseproof paper, overlapping them slightly, making a sheet big enough to wrap around the fillet. Spread the mushroom mixture lengthways over one half of the prosciutto, then sit the beef on top. Carefully roll up, tuck in the ends, then discard the paper. Secure with butcher's string.

Squash the remaining unpeeled garlic cloves and put into the roasting tray with the herbs, then carefully place the beef on top. Cook in the oven for 25 minutes for rare, 30 to 35 minutes for medium, or 40 minutes for well done. When the time's up, remove the meat to a board to rest for 5 minutes, pouring any juices back into the tray.

Transfer the tray to a medium-high heat on the hob, pour in the wine and the remaining porcini soaking liquor (discarding just the last gritty bit) and simmer to your desired consistency, scraping up all the goodness from the bottom of the tray. Remove from the heat, and sieve before serving, if you like – I also like to whisk in an extra knob of butter for maximum silkiness. Carve up the beef and serve drizzled with the red wine sauce – delicious with celeriac and potato mash, and steamed greens.

CALORIES	FAT	SAT FAT	PROTEIN	CARBS	SUGAR	SALT	FIBRE
439kcal	25.4g	12g	43g	2.8g	0.6g	1.4g	0.6g

Paloma Faith's

BACALHAU À BRÁS

PORTUGUESE SALT COD, POTATOES & EGGS

It may look a bit bonkers, but this traditional Portuguese dish of salt cod, scrambled eggs, fried potato matchsticks and marinated olives is the ultimate comfort food. Try it, and you'll never look back! You can find salt cod in some supermarkets now, otherwise get it online or from a good Portuguese deli.

PALOMA FAITH'S BACALHAU À BRÁS
PORTUGUESE SALT COD, POTATOES & EGGS

500g salt cod

1 bunch of fresh
  flat-leaf parsley (30g)

2 shallots

1 lemon

3 onions

olive oil

20 mixed-colour olives,
  stone in

1 pinch of dried chilli flakes

2 tablespoons red wine
  vinegar

extra virgin olive oil

500g Maris Piper potatoes

1.2 litres vegetable oil,
  for frying

6 large eggs

Place the salt cod in a large bowl and cover completely with cold water. Leave to soak for at least 12 hours, draining and covering with fresh water every few hours.

When you're ready to cook, finely slice the parsley stalks (reserving the leaves). Peel the shallots and finely slice into rounds. Using a speed-peeler, peel away strips of lemon zest. Place a large pan on a high heat, half fill with water and bring to the boil, then reduce to a simmer. Drain and add the salt cod, then the parsley stalks, shallots and lemon peel. Poach for around 20 minutes, or until the cod starts to soften and flake apart. Meanwhile, peel and finely slice the onions, then place in a large, wide pan on a medium heat with 2 tablespoons of olive oil. Season with black pepper and cook for 15 to 20 minutes, or until golden and starting to caramelize, stirring regularly. Destone the olives and tear the flesh into a bowl. Roughly chop the parsley leaves, and add half to the bowl with the chilli flakes, vinegar and 4 tablespoons of extra virgin olive oil. Mix well and set aside.

Use a slotted spoon to remove the salt cod to a plate. Pick out any bones, then break the flesh into the onion pan, also adding a good splash of poaching liquid. Cook for a further 10 minutes on a low heat, or until the fish is soft and flaking apart, stirring occasionally. Turn the heat off. Meanwhile, peel the potatoes, then finely slice into matchsticks using a mandolin (use the guard!) or a sharp knife. Just under half fill a sturdy pan with the vegetable oil – the oil should be 8cm deep, but never fill your pan more than half full – and place on a medium-high heat. Use a thermometer to tell when it's ready (170°C), or add a piece of potato and wait until it turns golden – that's the sign that it's ready to go. Working in batches, use a slotted spoon to carefully lower the potato matchsticks into the hot oil to cook for 1 to 2 minutes, or until very lightly golden, but not cooked through. Transfer to a double layer of kitchen paper to drain and repeat.

Return the cod mixture to a medium heat, then stir in most of the remaining chopped parsley. Beat the eggs, then gently stir them into the pan. Fold in three-quarters of the potato matchsticks and take the pan off the heat – the eggs will continue to cook in the pan, so make sure you don't overcook them at this stage. Return the remaining potato matchsticks to the hot oil to fry for a further 2 to 3 minutes, or until golden and cooked through. Transfer to a double layer of kitchen paper to drain, and season with sea salt.

Transfer the bacalhau to a serving dish and top with the crispy potato fries. Using a slotted spoon, spoon over the marinated olives, then sprinkle the remaining chopped parsley on top. Great served with a green salad and a cold glass of dry white wine.

CALORIES	FAT	SAT FAT	PROTEIN	CARBS	SUGAR	SALT	FIBRE
433kcal	28g	4.5g	25.1g	22.1g	5.9g	3g	2.8g

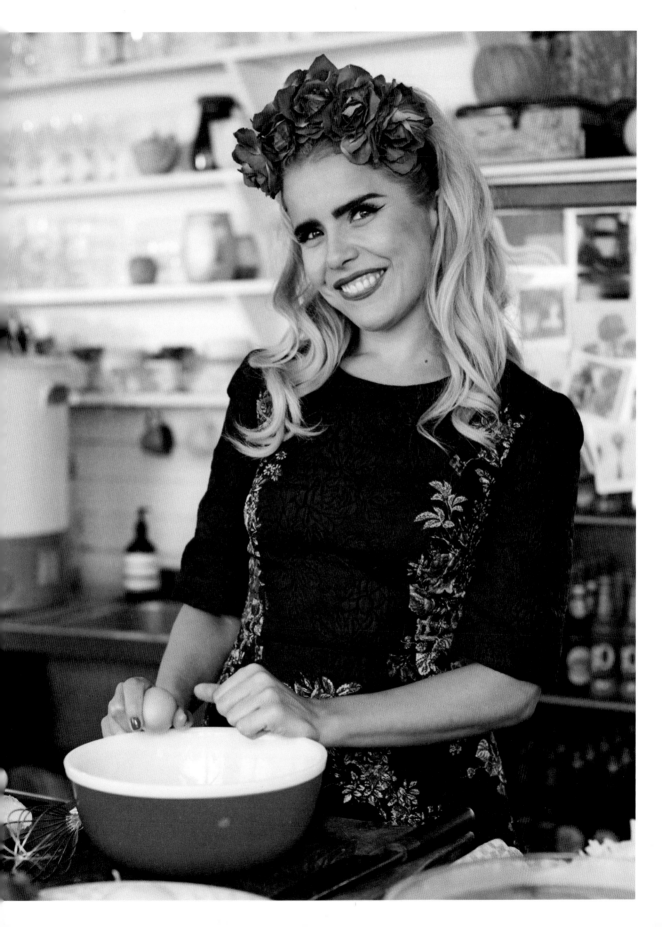

PRAWN & TOFU PAD THAI

TANGY TAMARIND SAUCE & DRIED SHRIMPS

SERVES 2 | TOTAL TIME - 40 MINUTES

Pad Thai has become a bit of a cult favourite in both street food markets and high-end Thai restaurants, and it's not hard to see why – it's ridiculously tasty and seriously satisfying. Packed with proper Thai flavours like dried shrimps, Asian herbs and a beautiful tamarind sauce, it's fresh and zingy but hearty and warming – a modern classic.

150g flat rice noodles

1 fresh bird's-eye chilli

1 fresh yellow chilli

2 limes

groundnut oil

2 red shallots

½ a bunch each of Chinese chives, Thai basil, Thai mint (45g total)

140g silken tofu

4 large raw peeled tiger prawns

25g dried shrimps

50g shelled unsalted peanuts

1 pinch of dried chilli flakes

1 tablespoon jarred shredded sweet radish

1 large egg

60g beansprouts

TAMARIND SAUCE

25g palm sugar

2 tablespoons tamarind paste

fish sauce

white wine vinegar

Cook the rice noodles according to the packet instructions. Meanwhile, make the tamarind sauce. Coarsely grate the palm sugar into a bowl, add the tamarind paste, 1 tablespoon of fish sauce, a dash of vinegar and 2 tablespoons of boiling water and mix well so the sugar dissolves. Taste, and adjust the flavours if needed – you're looking for sweet, sour and slightly salty. Halve, deseed and finely slice the chillies, then place in a bowl with the juice from 1 lime to make a quick pickle.

Drain the noodles and toss in a little oil. Peel and roughly chop the shallots, then trim and finely slice the chives. Pick and roughly chop most of the basil and mint leaves. Slice the tofu into rough 1cm chunks. Run the tip of a knife down the back of each prawn and pull out the vein, meaning they'll butterfly as they cook. Rinse the dried shrimps under cold running water, then pat dry with kitchen paper.

Place a large wok on a medium heat with a splash of oil, then add the dried shrimps, peanuts and chilli flakes. Toss for 2 to 3 minutes, or until golden. Take the pan off the heat, transfer half the mixture to a pestle and mortar and lightly crush, keeping to one side. Return the pan to a medium-high heat with another splash of oil, adding the shallots to the mix. Fry for 2 minutes, or until turning golden. Toss in the prawns, chives, chopped herbs and shredded radish, then cook for a further 2 to 3 minutes, or until the prawns are almost cooked through. Beat and add the egg, cook for 1 to 2 minutes, then fold through and toss in the tofu, noodles, beansprouts and tamarind sauce until well combined.

Divide the pad Thai between bowls, sprinkle over the crushed nut mixture from the mortar and pick over the remaining mint and basil leaves. Serve with the quick pickled chillies and lime wedges for squeezing over. Delicious!

CALORIES	FAT	SAT FAT	PROTEIN	CARBS	SUGAR	SALT	FIBRE
661kcal	20.2g	4g	28.9g	89.6g	16.9g	1.2g	2.6g

EPIC POACHED CHICKEN & DUMPLINGS

MUSTARD SAUCE & FIERY HORSERADISH

· **SERVES 8 | TOTAL TIME – 2 HOURS 20 MINUTES** ·

If you're after a pick-me-up bowlful of steaming goodness, this clean, delicate but wonderfully comforting dish, inspired by the classic Jewish penicillin, is hard to beat. Breaking with tradition, I've added a cheeky twist by super-charging it with two punchy condiments – if you're kosher, use straight-up horseradish instead.

1 x 2kg whole chicken

5 juniper berries

1 bulb of fennel

2 large carrots

8 baby carrots

1 onion

1 celery heart

1 bunch of mixed herbs, such as rosemary, thyme, tarragon (30g)

1 bulb of garlic

250g fine egg noodles

250g fresh or frozen podded peas

250g fresh or frozen podded broad beans

extra virgin olive oil

DUMPLINGS

4 large eggs

5 tablespoons chicken fat (from the poached chicken)

120g medium matzo meal, plus extra for dusting

Place the chicken in a large, deep pot with the juniper berries and 1 teaspoon of sea salt, then cover with cold water. Pop the lid on and simmer over a medium heat for 1 hour 30 minutes, skimming away and discarding any scum and froth, and reserving any fat that rises to the surface. Trim the fennel and chop into 8 wedges, reserving any herby tops for later. Scrub and trim the carrots, roughly chopping the large ones, then peel and quarter the onion, and trim and roughly chop the celery, reserving any delicate yellow leaves. When the time's up on the chicken, tie the herbs together and add to the pot with the bulb of garlic and all the veg, except the peas and broad beans. Cook for 30 minutes, or until the veg are perfectly cooked and the chicken is falling away from the bone.

Meanwhile, make the dumplings. Beat the eggs with 5 tablespoons of the reserved chicken fat, then stir in the matzo meal and a pinch of salt and black pepper – the dough should be quite sticky. You want to make about 24 dumplings, so, with wet hands, form 3cm to 4cm balls,

placing them on a large tray lined with greaseproof paper as you go. Firm up in the fridge until needed.

Once done, carefully transfer the chicken and veg to a large bowl. Pour the broth through a sieve into a large shallow pan (big enough to fit the dumplings in a single layer), then taste and season to perfection. Bring to the boil, then dot in the dumplings. Cook for 5 minutes, then add the noodles, peas and broad beans, and cook for a further 5 minutes. Meanwhile, pull the chicken off the bone in big chunks, discarding any bones and skin, then arrange nicely on a serving platter with all the veg, ladling over a little of the cooking liquor to stop it from drying out. Drizzle with oil, then scatter over most of the remaining fennel tops and the reserved celery leaves.

Serve steaming ladles of chicken broth with the dumplings, noodles, peas and broad beans. Top generously with shredded poached chicken and veg. Finish with Mustard sauce and Fiery horseradish (see page 161), to taste.

CALORIES	FAT	SAT FAT	PROTEIN	CARBS	SUGAR	SALT	FIBRE
501kcal	16.7g	4.7g	41.4g	48.5g	6.5g	1.3g	5.9g

THESE VALUES INCLUDE THE CONDIMENTS

MUSTARD SAUCE

· ·

4 teaspoons English
    mustard powder

2 tablespoons white
    wine vinegar

Mix the mustard powder, vinegar and a good pinch of salt and pepper together in a little
bowl, then sprinkle over the reserved herby fennel tops from the chicken recipe.

FIERY HORSERADISH

· ·

35g fresh horseradish

½ a lemon

100g half-fat crème fraîche

extra virgin olive oil

Peel the horseradish and finely grate into a little bowl with the lemon zest, then squeeze in
the juice. Stir in the crème fraîche, drizzle over a little oil, season and mix well.

JAMAICAN-STYLE JERK PORK

GOLDEN YAMS & HOMEMADE DUMPLINGS

This is an unbelievable plate of food inspired by the fantastic tastes of Jamaica – fiery chillies, fragrant spices and, of course, dark Jamaican rum. Making the jerk sauce from scratch creates smells and flavours you won't believe, and I'm serving it all up with proper Jamaican yams and dumplings. Comfort food at its best.

dark Jamaican rum

olive oil

2kg pork belly,
   skin removed

10 fresh bay leaves

2 medium onions

1.4kg yellow yams

1 large knob of
   unsalted butter

250g self-raising flour,
   plus extra for dusting

50g cornmeal

JERK SAUCE

8 spring onions

8 cloves of garlic

2 fresh Scotch bonnet
   chillies

½ a bunch of fresh
   thyme (15g)

3 fresh bay leaves

½ teaspoon ground cloves

1 teaspoon ground allspice

1 teaspoon ground nutmeg

6 tablespoons white wine
   vinegar

2 tablespoons runny honey

To make the jerk sauce, trim and roughly chop the spring onions, peel the garlic, deseed the chillies and place it all in a blender. Strip in the thyme leaves, then tear in the bay leaves, discarding the stalks. Add the remaining sauce ingredients and a splash of rum. Blitz until smooth, loosening with a little oil, if needed. Massage half the jerk sauce into the pork belly, then cover and marinate in the fridge for at least 2 hours, preferably overnight.

When you're ready to cook, preheat the oven to 150°C/300°F/gas 2. Place a large, wide, ovenproof pan on a medium-high heat with 1 tablespoon of oil. Chop the pork into 5cm chunks and add to the pan with 3 bay leaves. Cook for 10 to 15 minutes, or until the pork is golden all over and any liquid has bubbled and boiled away. Peel, finely slice and add the onions, then cook on a low heat for 10 minutes, or until soft and sticky. Turn the heat up to high, add a good splash of rum and allow to bubble away, then stir in the remaining jerk sauce and 250ml of water. Bring to the boil, then cover and cook in the oven for 3 to 4 hours, or until sticky and reduced and the meat is tender, adding a splash of water if it's too dry. You want it nice and juicy, but it's not a stew!

With around 25 minutes to go, peel the yams and chop into rough 2cm chunks. Parboil in a pan of boiling salted water for 10 minutes, then drain and allow to steam dry. Place in a large ovenproof frying pan on a medium-high heat with the butter, a good drizzle of oil and the remaining bay leaves. Fry for 10 minutes, or until golden. Meanwhile, remove the pork from the oven, cover and put aside, then turn the temperature up to 200°C/400°F/gas 6. Transfer the yams to the oven for 15 minutes, or until crisp and cooked through.

Make the dumplings by mixing the flour, cornmeal, a good pinch of sea salt and 250ml of cold water to form a sticky dough. Knead well on a flour-dusted surface, then roll into a sausage shape and tear off golfball-sized pieces. Roll into balls, flatten slightly with your hands, then place in a pan of boiling salted water for 15 minutes, or until puffed up and cooked through, turning occasionally. Drain and serve with the jerk pork and crispy yams.

CALORIES	FAT	SAT FAT	PROTEIN	CARBS	SUGAR	SALT	FIBRE
810kcal	30.1g	10.8g	56.7g	82.2g	9.3g	1g	4.1g

GURKHA CHICKEN CURRY

FRAGRANT YOGHURT MARINADE

SERVES 8 | TOTAL TIME – 1 HOUR 45 MINUTES, PLUS MARINATING

Swap your usual Friday night takeaway for this amazing and comforting homemade chicken curry. It's fresh, fragrant, crammed with flavour, and the charred chicken is so ridiculously tender it falls right off the bone. Everyone needs to try this super-tasty Gurkha curry – trust me, it's happiness guaranteed and people go mad for it.

8 large chicken thighs,
  skin on, bone in

1 large onion

3 potatoes

4 large ripe tomatoes

½ a bunch of fresh
  coriander (15g)

vegetable oil

1 stick of cinnamon

4 cloves

1 teaspoon cumin seeds

3 fresh bay leaves

1 teaspoon ground
  turmeric

1 tablespoon ground
  coriander

optional: 1 fresh red chilli

MARINADE

5cm piece of ginger

1 bulb of garlic

1 teaspoon fennel seeds

5 cardamom pods

1 teaspoon hot
  chilli powder

1 lemon

250ml fat-free natural
  yoghurt

To make the marinade, peel and roughly slice the ginger, peel the garlic cloves, then place in a dry frying pan on a medium heat with the fennel seeds and cardamom pods. Leave for 1 minute to wake up all those lovely flavours, then tip into a pestle and mortar. Pound to a rough paste with the chilli powder and a pinch of sea salt. Transfer to a large sealable bag, finely grate in the lemon zest, squeeze in the juice and add the yoghurt. Remove the chicken skin, then place in the bag, seal and massage to coat. Marinate in the fridge for at least 1 hour, preferably overnight.

Preheat the oven to 190°C/375°F/gas 5. Peel and finely chop the onion. Peel the potatoes, then chop into rough chunks with the tomatoes. Finely chop the coriander stalks (reserving the leaves). Place a large, wide ovenproof pan on a medium heat with 4 tablespoons of oil, the cinnamon, cloves, cumin seeds and bay. Add the chicken in a single layer with its marinade and cook for 5 minutes on one side, or until a lovely golden crust develops. Stir in the ground spices, then add the onion, potatoes, tomatoes and coriander stalks. Turn the chicken and cook for a further 5 to 10 minutes, or until browned all over. Pour over 350ml of cold water, then bring to the boil. Transfer to the oven for 50 minutes to 1 hour, or until the chicken is tender, stirring occasionally.

Pick out and discard the cinnamon and any visible cardamom pods, then finely slice and sprinkle over the chilli (if using). Tear over the coriander leaves and serve. Great with a dollop of yoghurt, coconut rice, naan breads and a fresh green salad.

CALORIES	FAT	SAT FAT	PROTEIN	CARBS	SUGAR	SALT	FIBRE
249kcal	12.6g	2.2g	19.2g	17.4g	6g	0.5g	1.8g

Goldie Hawn's
FETTUCCINE ALFREDO

FINISHED WITH FRESH TRUFFLE OR NUTMEG

· · · · · · · · · · SERVES 4 | TOTAL TIME – 45 MINUTES, PLUS RESTING · · · · · · · · · ·

Homemade pasta, in a silky sauce of double cream, Parmesan and fresh truffle (or nutmeg, which is easier to get hold of and just as tasty!) is a well-known Italian dish that I cooked up for Goldie – she loves it! This is my take, swapping in some single cream to make it a little less naughty. Trust me, it's still a heavenly mouthful.

GOLDIE HAWN'S FETTUCCINE ALFREDO
FINISHED WITH FRESH TRUFFLE OR NUTMEG

½ x Royal pasta dough
  (see page 244)

fine semolina, for dusting

150ml double cream

150ml single cream

1 large egg

60g Parmesan cheese,
  plus extra to serve

1 fresh truffle or 1 whole
  nutmeg, for grating

truffle oil

Make the Royal pasta dough (see page 244). Once it's relaxed for 30 minutes, roll the sheets out to 2mm thick. Set up the fettuccine attachment on your pasta machine and gently run through each pasta sheet, placing on a semolina-dusted tray as you go. Or, if making by hand, loosely roll up the pasta sheets, cut into strips just over ½cm wide, then use your fingertips to shake out and separate into strands.

When ready, cook the fettuccine in a large pan of boiling salted water for 1 to 2 minutes, or until al dente. Meanwhile, gently heat all the cream in a large frying pan on a low heat, then separate the egg and whisk the yolk into the pan (save the white for another day). Finely grate and gently whisk in the Parmesan, then season with sea salt and black pepper.

Using tongs, drag the pasta straight into the sauce, taking a little cooking water with it. Toss together, adding extra splashes of cooking water to loosen into a lovely, silky sauce, if needed. Plate up with fine gratings of truffle or nutmeg and a good grating of Parmesan, drizzle with a little truffle oil and serve right away.

CALORIES	FAT	SAT FAT	PROTEIN	CARBS	SUGAR	SALT	FIBRE
612kcal	38.5g	19.8g	22.8g	44.7g	3g	0.6g	1.7g

BEAUTIFUL STUFFED PORCHETTA

EPIC CRACKLING & HOMEMADE GRAVY

• • • • • SERVES 20 | TOTAL TIME – 6 HOURS 30 MINUTES, PLUS COOLING • • • • •

When you've got a big crowd to feed, this recipe is sure to go down an absolute treat. With crispy crackling and rich, fennel-spiked liver stuffing, it makes the perfect Sunday lunch with all the trimmings, or you could serve it up with baps, slaw and an array of condiments for a build-your-own party centrepiece.

BEAUTIFUL STUFFED PORCHETTA
EPIC CRACKLING & HOMEMADE GRAVY

1 x 5kg pork loin with belly attached, skin on (ask your butcher to remove the bones, butterfly open the loin meat and score the skin vertically at ½cm intervals)

3 eating apples

4 carrots

2 red onions

2 heaped tablespoons plain flour

500ml quality chicken stock

STUFFING

4 large red onions

1 bunch of fresh sage (30g)

olive oil

1 knob of unsalted butter

75g pine nuts

1 heaped teaspoon fennel seeds

75g raisins

250ml Vin Santo

170g sourdough bread

1 clove of garlic

2 sprigs of fresh rosemary

150g chicken or pork livers, cleaned

1 lemon

8 fresh oysters

30g Parmesan cheese

Place the pork loin on a board, skin side down, and rub all over with a good pinch of sea salt and black pepper. To make the stuffing, peel and finely slice the onions, then pick and chop the sage leaves. Place a large pan on a medium-low heat with 1 tablespoon of oil and the butter, then add the onions, sage, pine nuts, fennel seeds and a pinch of salt and pepper. Cook for 25 to 30 minutes, or until soft and lightly golden, stirring occasionally. Meanwhile, place the raisins and Vin Santo in a bowl and set aside to soak. Slice the sourdough and toast until golden, then halve the garlic clove and rub the cut side all over the toast. Pick the rosemary leaves and finely chop with the toast. Roughly chop the livers and stir into the pan. Turn the heat up to medium-high, stir in the soaked raisins, Vin Santo and toast, then finely grate in the lemon zest. Transfer to a bowl and leave to cool. Preheat the oven to 220°C/425°F/gas 7.

Once cool, use clean hands to scrunch the mixture together, then scatter over the pork. Hold the oysters curved side down on a chopping board, look for the hinge between the top and bottom shell, then poke an oyster knife into the crack and prise it open (it's not always easy, so you'll need to use force here – but please be careful!). Press the oysters into the filling, and drizzle over any juices. Finely grate over the Parmesan, then, starting with one of the shortest edges, roll up the pork, patting on and compacting the stuffing as you go. Tie six pieces of string along the rolled meat to secure it, with the seam underneath, then season well and drizzle with oil, rubbing it all over the skin – this will help you get delicious crackling. Put the pork into a large roasting tray and place in the oven for 30 to 40 minutes, or until the skin is crisp and crackled. Meanwhile, halve the apples and carrots, then peel and quarter the onions. Remove the pork from the oven and carefully place the apples and veg underneath the pork in the tray, then return to the oven and reduce the temperature to 180°C/350°F/gas 4. Cook for a further 4 to 5 hours, or until the meat is really tender, basting now and again.

Remove the porchetta to a clean tray and leave to rest while you make the gravy. Place the roasting tray on a medium heat on the hob. Skim away most of the fat from the surface into a jar, cool, and place in the fridge for another day. Stir in the flour, scraping up all those gnarly bits from the bottom of the tray. Pour in the stock and bring to the boil for 5 minutes, or until thickened, stirring occasionally. Strain through a sieve, pushing through all the goodness with the back of a spoon. Remove the string from the porchetta and carve. Serve with the homemade gravy and all the trimmings.

CALORIES	FAT	SAT FAT	PROTEIN	CARBS	SUGAR	SALT	FIBRE
689kcal	48.6g	16.8g	46.2g	15.6g	8.6g	1g	1.6g

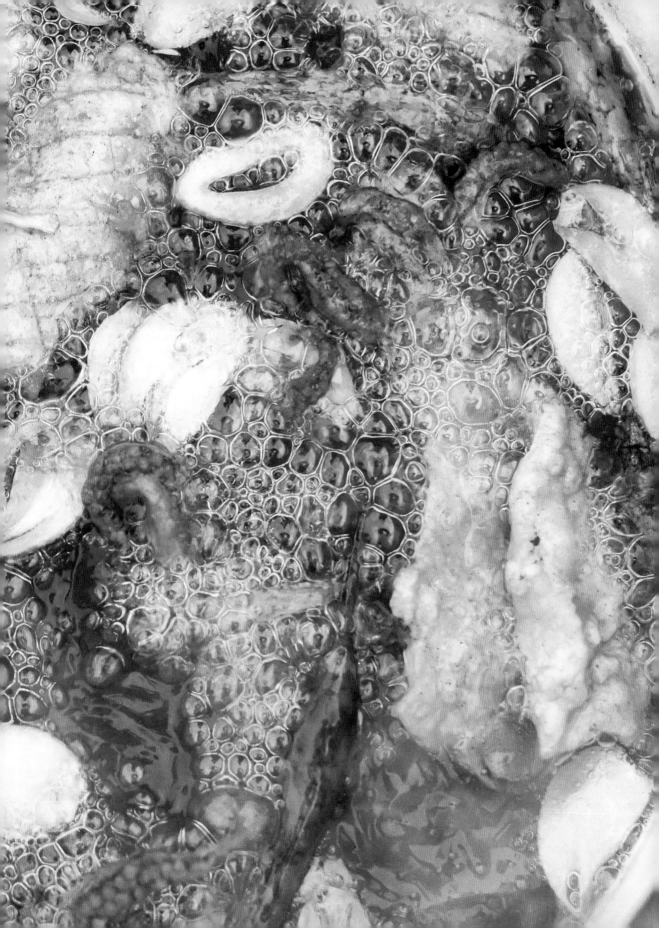

SALT & PEPPER SQUID

LITTLE RAYS OF SUNSHINE

Crispy but tender squid with a hum of pepper heat, complemented by fragrant herbs, crispy garlic and a hit of vinegar – this is my evolution of the classic dish that I know you all love. Traditionally, it comes from Cantonese cuisine, where heat was achieved using finely ground peppercorns, but I couldn't resist adding a few chillies here for double pleasure.

½ a bunch of fresh
  mint (15g)

4 spring onions

8 medium whole squid
  (500g), gutted, cleaned

vegetable oil, for frying

white pepper

100g plain flour

1 small handful of fresh
  mixed-colour chillies

4 cloves of garlic

1 tablespoon white
  or red wine vinegar

Pick the mint leaves into a small bowl of cold water to ensure they stay super-fresh. Trim the spring onions and halve across the middle, then finely slice lengthways and add to the water bowl. Pat the squid dry with kitchen paper, then use a regular eating knife to lightly score the inside of the squid at ½cm intervals at an angle. Turn the squid through 90° and do the same again to create a criss-cross pattern.

When you're ready to cook, just under half fill a large sturdy pan with oil – the oil should be 8cm deep, but never fill your pan more than half full – and place on a medium-high heat. Use a thermometer to tell when it's ready (170°C), or add a piece of potato and wait until it turns golden – that's the sign that it's ready to go. While it heats, tip 1 heaped tablespoon of white pepper and the flour into a large bowl with a pinch of sea salt. Add the squid, toss and mix together to coat, then leave in the flour for a few minutes while you prick the chillies – if some are bigger, halve and deseed them first – then peel and finely slice the garlic 1mm thick, ideally on a mandolin (use the guard!).

When you're ready to fry, add half the squid and chillies – it's important to cook in two batches so you don't overcrowd the pan. When it's all looking golden and lovely (after about 1½ minutes), add half the garlic for a final minute. Use a slotted spoon to scoop everything into a bowl or pan lined with kitchen paper to drain while you cook the second batch. Whip out the paper, then cut the squid into bite-sized pieces and return to the bowl. Drizzle with the vinegar, add a good pinch of seasoning, the drained mint leaves and spring onion curls, toss it all together and serve right away.

CALORIES	FAT	SAT FAT	PROTEIN	CARBS	SUGAR	SALT	FIBRE
343kcal	18.7g	2.4g	22.6g	22.6g	1g	1.4g	1.1g

Gary Barlow's
SCRUMPTIOUS STEAK & STOUT PIES

MELTED CHEDDAR & RICH CRUMBLY PASTRY

SERVES 10 | TOTAL TIME – 3 HOURS

Wednesday night was pie night for Gary growing up, but I think this pie recipe is just perfect for a Friday night extravaganza. Using beef skirt gives a ridiculously tender filling, and adding a cheeky grating of Cheddar that melts under the short, crumbly pastry as the pie cooks makes this a really phenomenal eating experience.

GARY BARLOW'S SCRUMPTIOUS STEAK & STOUT PIES
MELTED CHEDDAR & RICH CRUMBLY PASTRY

olive oil

1 knob of unsalted butter

3 red onions

3 sprigs of fresh rosemary

3 sprigs of fresh thyme

3 fresh bay leaves

1kg beef skirt

750g chestnut mushrooms

2 tablespoons tomato
    purée

3 tablespoons balsamic
    vinegar

300ml stout or dark ale

3 heaped tablespoons
    plain flour

750ml quality beef stock

80g Westcombe Cheddar

1 large egg

PASTRY

300g plain flour, plus extra
    for dusting

100g shredded suet

100g unsalted butter (cold)

Place a large casserole pan on a medium heat with 2 tablespoons of oil and the butter. Peel, finely slice and add the onions, then pick, finely chop and add the rosemary and thyme, along with the bay leaves. Cook for 20 minutes, or until the onions are soft and turning golden, stirring occasionally. Slice the beef into rough 2cm strips, then clean and slice the mushrooms. Add both to the pan along with the tomato purée and a good pinch of sea salt and black pepper. Stir in the balsamic, stout, flour and stock and bring to the boil. Reduce the heat to low, cover, and simmer for 1 hour 20 minutes, or until the sauce has thickened and the meat is tender.

Meanwhile, for the pastry, put the flour and a good pinch of salt into a bowl with the suet, cube and add the butter, then use your thumb and forefingers to rub the fat into the flour until it resembles coarse breadcrumbs. Slowly stir in 125ml of ice-cold water, then use your hands to gently bring it together into a ball, but don't overwork it. Wrap in clingfilm and place in the fridge for later.

Preheat the oven to 180°C/350°F/gas 4. Ladle the stew into pie dishes – you can make a collection of small pies, or one or two larger ones – then finely grate or crumble over the cheese. Roll out the pastry on a clean flour-dusted surface, so it's slightly bigger than your pie dishes. Eggwash the edges of the dishes, then carefully place the pastry on top, trimming off any overhang. Pinch the edges to seal. Decorate the tops with any offcuts, if you like, then brush with a little more egg. Bake for 45 to 50 minutes, or until the pastry is beautifully golden. Delicious served with steamed seasonal greens.

CALORIES	FAT	SAT FAT	PROTEIN	CARBS	SUGAR	SALT	FIBRE
552kcal	33g	15g	26.6g	37.6g	7.4g	0.7g	3.2g

SALT-CRUST SALMON

FENNEL, LEMON & HERBS GALORE

Baking salmon in a salt crust creates a natural cave that helps the salmon retain maximum moisture as it cooks, as well as imparting a very delicate seasoning. It's not only a showstopper, you'll get the most perfectly cooked flaky fish, too.

1 x 2kg whole salmon, gutted, gills removed, scales left on

4 lemons

1 bulb of fennel

½ a bunch of fresh flat-leaf parsley (15g)

½ a bunch of fresh marjoram (15g)

1 bunch of fresh chives (30g)

4kg rock salt

2 large eggs

BASIL YOGHURT

½ a bunch of fresh basil (15g)

1 teaspoon English mustard

500g Greek yoghurt

extra virgin olive oil

CHILLI SALSA

3 fresh red chillies

1 bunch of fresh mint (30g)

runny honey

cider vinegar

Preheat the oven to 180°C/350°F/gas 4. Wash the salmon well both inside and out, then pat dry with kitchen paper. Finely slice 1 lemon and the fennel into rounds and stuff into the salmon cavity with the parsley, marjoram and chives.

Combine the rock salt, eggs and 250ml of water in a large bowl, then evenly spread one-third of the mixture over a large baking tray (35cm x 45cm). Make a slight hollow in the middle to hold the salmon snugly, lay the salmon diagonally in the tray, then spoon over the remaining salt mixture, heaping it around and on to the salmon to create an even 2cm-thick layer all over the fish. Bake for 35 minutes. To test if the salmon is ready, push a skewer through the salt into the thickest part of the fish – if it comes out warm after 5 seconds, it's done. Remove from the oven and set aside in the crust for just 1 hour.

Meanwhile, make the basil yoghurt. Pick the basil leaves into a blender and add the mustard, the juice of 1 lemon and half the yoghurt. Blitz until smooth, then fold back through the rest of the yoghurt with 4 tablespoons of oil, and season to perfection with sea salt and black pepper. To make the salsa, deseed the chillies and very finely chop with the mint leaves and a drizzle of honey. Scrape into a bowl, add 2 tablespoons of oil and 2 teaspoons of vinegar, and season to perfection.

Lightly crack the salt casing and pull it away from the salmon, brushing any excess from the top. Gently loosen and carefully transfer the fish to a large platter. Pull the skin away, then use a regular eating knife to scrape away any darker fish, leaving you with beautifully cooked pink salmon, which you can rustically remove in flakes and lobes. Serve with the basil yoghurt, salsa and lemon wedges for squeezing over.

CALORIES	FAT	SAT FAT	PROTEIN	CARBS	SUGAR	SALT	FIBRE
629kcal	43g	10.3g	55g	5.4g	4.8g	1.7g	1.2g

Josh Hartnett's
PORK RAMEN
CHICKEN BROTH & SOY-ROASTED PORK BELLY

•••••• SERVES 6 | TOTAL TIME – 4 HOURS 30 MINUTES, PLUS MARINATING ••••••

Josh is a bit of a ramen addict, and has a favourite noodle bar in almost every city he's been to! While it seems simple and comforting, homemade ramen is serious business. This isn't a dish for the faint-hearted, but the flavour that you get from carefully making all the different pieces of the puzzle and bringing them together in one beautiful bowlful is really mind-blowing. I hope you enjoy!

JOSH HARTNETT'S PORK RAMEN
CHICKEN BROTH & SOY-ROASTED PORK BELLY

1 x Marinated eggs
(see page 188)

1 x Ramen noodles
(see page 189) or 450g
dried ramen noodles

PORK BELLY CHASHU

750g pork belly, skin off

10g coarse kosher salt

20g soft light brown sugar

30ml low-salt soy sauce

APPLE SOFFRITTO

1 onion

4 cloves of garlic

3cm piece of ginger

1 tart green apple

1 tablespoon canola
or rapeseed oil

SHOYU TARE

75ml sake

75ml mirin

100ml low-salt soy sauce

BROTH

1 litre quality chicken stock

1 litre dashi

GARNISHES

3 spring onions

1 fresh red chilli

The day before you're going to cook, make the Marinated eggs (see page 188) and prep the pork. Sit the pork in a tray, sprinkle with the kosher salt and the sugar, drizzle over the soy, then rub all over. Cover and marinate in the fridge overnight.

The next day, preheat the oven to 160°C/325°F/gas 3. Remove the pork from the marinade, brushing off the excess salt and sugar. Place in a snug-fitting roasting tray, cover with tin foil and roast for 4 hours, or until super-tender, reserving the fat from the tray. Meanwhile, make the Ramen noodles (see page 189). For the apple soffritto, peel and very finely chop the onion, garlic, ginger and apple (discarding the core). Place in a pan with the oil on a low heat and fry gently for 45 minutes, or until softened but not coloured, stirring regularly, then remove from the heat.

For the shoyu tare, pour the sake and mirin into a pan and bring to the boil on a high heat. Leave to bubble away for 4 minutes, then reduce the heat to low, add the soy and apple soffritto, cook for an additional 5 minutes, then remove from the heat.

When you're getting ready to serve, make your broth: bring the stock and dashi to the boil in a large pan, then simmer over a medium heat for 5 minutes. Put a pan of water on to boil for the noodels, then thinly slice the pork.

Get yourself six warm bowls. Spoon 1 tablespoon each of the shoyu tare and reserved pork fat into the bowls, then divide up the broth. Cook the noodles in the pan of boiling water for 45 seconds (or according to the packet instructions), then remove, shaking off any excess water. Divide between the bowls, using chopsticks to separate, if needed. Top each bowl with slices of pork and a halved marinated egg. Trim and finely slice the spring onions and chilli (deseed if you like), and scatter over the top to finish.

CALORIES	FAT	SAT FAT	PROTEIN	CARBS	SUGAR	SALT	FIBRE
349kcal	15.9g	4.8g	32.1g	19.7g	13g	3.5g	1g

MARINATED EGGS

SOY, SAKE, HONEY & GINGER

· · · · · · · · · · · · · · · · · · · MAKES 6 | TOTAL TIME - 20 MINUTES, PLUS MARINATING ·

These eggs are the classic way to finish any ramen. They're soft-boiled, but then the yolks gently set while they sit in their soy and honey bath overnight, so when you cut into them they're deliciously jammy in texture. A top ramen tip – don't halve the eggs with a knife, use a wire to get that perfectly clean cross-section.

6 large eggs

5cm piece of ginger

1 clove of garlic

80ml low-salt soy sauce

50ml sake

1 tablespoon runny honey

Cook the eggs in a pan of boiling salted water over a medium heat for 5½ minutes exactly, then remove to a bowl of iced water to stop them cooking further. Peel and finely slice the ginger and smash the garlic, then place in a heavy-bottomed pan with the soy sauce and sake. Bring to the boil over a medium heat, then cook for 5 minutes. Stir in the honey and remove from the heat. Leave to infuse for 3 minutes, then strain and reserve the liquid. Stir 500ml of cold water into the reserved liquid. Carefully peel the eggs, then add to the marinade and leave to infuse in the fridge for 24 hours, removing the eggs from the marinade when you're ready to serve.

CALORIES	FAT	SAT FAT	PROTEIN	CARBS	SUGAR	SALT	FIBRE
83kcal	6.2g	1.7g	7.2g	0.4g	0.3g	0.3g	0g

RAMEN NOODLES
MADE WITH TOASTED RYE FLOUR

The perfect ramen noodle should be springy and elastic (this is what the kansui powder does – see tip), allowing the rich, salty broth to cling to it. Although they're quite hands-on to make, once you get into the noodle-making zone, it's surprisingly therapeutic to knock out a few portions. Knowing you've made them from scratch is really satisfying.

40g rye flour

300g strong white flour

150g plain flour

1 teaspoon kansui powder (see tip)

cornflour, for dusting

To really wake up the flavours, toast the rye flour in a large dry pan over a medium heat for 4 minutes, but don't let it colour. Place in the bowl of a freestanding mixer, then combine with the other flours. Dissolve the kansui powder and 1 teaspoon of sea salt in 420ml of cold water. Gradually add the water to the flours, slowly beginning to beat with the dough hook. Once incorporated, beat on high for 10 minutes, or until it starts to come together into a grainy dough (it shouldn't feel sticky). Wrap in clingfilm and place in the fridge to chill for 1 hour.

When you're ready to roll, cut off a manageable piece of dough. Cover the rest with a clean damp tea towel while you work, to stop it drying out. Using a pasta machine, roll the piece of dough through the widest setting. Fold the edges of the dough back into the middle and roll through again, then work down through the settings until the sheets are 1–2mm thick. Switch attachments and cut into 1–2mm-thick noodles, tossing them in cornflour as you go. Repeat with the remaining dough. To cook, simply plunge them into a pan of boiling water for 45 seconds, then remove, shaking off any excess water.

> If you can't get hold of kansui powder, simply scatter a thin layer of bicarbonate of soda over a lined baking tray, and bake for 1 hour at 120°C/250°F/gas ½. Leave to cool, then store in an airtight container until needed.

CALORIES	FAT	SAT FAT	PROTEIN	CARBS	SUGAR	SALT	FIBRE
278kcal	1.1g	0.2g	7.6g	63.4g	1.2g	0.9g	3.3g

VEAL RAGÙ CANNELLONI

MELTY CHEESE, BUTTON MUSHROOMS & GARLICKY GREENS

· · · · · · · · · · · SERVES 8 | TOTAL TIME - 3 HOURS 50 MINUTES · · · · · · · · · ·

This is cannelloni, but not like you've seen it before! Good British rose veal is a really smart and sustainable choice of meat that's chronically underused here in the UK and is super-delicious. Although it will be a struggle, it's important to let the cannelloni rest after baking before tucking in – be patient!

VEAL RAGÙ CANNELLONI
MELTY CHEESE, BUTTON MUSHROOMS & GARLICKY GREENS

2 onions

2 sticks of celery

4 cloves of garlic

2 medium leeks

500g Maris Piper potatoes

½ a bunch of fresh
  thyme (15g)

40g unsalted butter

olive oil

4 fresh bay leaves

500g minced rose veal

500g minced pork shoulder

300ml white wine

1 whole nutmeg,
  for grating

2 tablespoons plain flour

2 litres semi-skimmed milk

½ teaspoon dried
  red chilli flakes

500g stinging nettles

500g baby spinach

240g mixed cheese,
  such as Cheddar,
  Lancashire, Berkswell

250g dried cannelloni tubes

200g button mushrooms

Preheat the oven to 160°C/325°F/gas 3. Peel and finely chop the onions, celery and 2 cloves of garlic. Cut the green part off the leeks (save for making stock or soup), then trim, wash and finely chop the white part. Peel the potatoes and chop into ½cm dice. Tie the thyme sprigs together. Melt half the butter in a large pan on a low heat with 1 tablespoon of oil, then add the onions, garlic, celery, leeks, potatoes, bay leaves and thyme. Cover and sweat down for 15 minutes, or until softened, stirring occasionally.

Add all the mince to the pan, breaking it up with a wooden spoon. Turn the heat up to medium-high and cook for 10 more minutes, or until the mince is browned all over, stirring occasionally. Pour in the wine, let it bubble and boil away, then finely grate in half the nutmeg. Stir in the flour for 1 minute, then pour in the milk. Season with sea salt and black pepper, cover with a scrunched-up sheet of wet greaseproof paper and transfer to the oven for 2 hours, or until thickened and beautifully tender. At this stage, the ragù might look like it's split a little, but this is actually what we're looking for – the milk in the sauce creates amazing ricotta-like curds as it cooks.

Meanwhile, place a large heatproof baking dish on a medium heat with 2 tablespoons of oil and the remaining butter. Peel, finely chop and add the remaining garlic, along with the chilli flakes, nettles (leaves only – wear gloves to protect your hands while you prep) and spinach – you'll need to work in batches. Cook for 10 minutes, or until softened. Allow to cool, then finely chop and return to the dish, spreading evenly over the base. Once done, divide the ragù in two, freezing one half for another day, once cool. Carefully drain the liquid from the remaining ragù into a bowl through a coarse sieve. Return the ragù to the pan, fish out and discard the thyme stalks and bay, then grate in half the cheese and stir well. Turn the oven up to 180°C/350°F/gas 4.

Use a piping bag or teaspoon to stuff the cannelloni tubes with the ragù, then arrange on top of the greens. Pour the sieved liquid over the top and grate over the remaining cheese. Trim and finely slice the mushrooms and scatter over the cannelloni. Drizzle with 1 tablespoon of oil, then bake for 40 to 45 minutes, or until golden and bubbling. For added colour, flash the dish under the grill for 5 minutes. Importantly, let it stand for 30 minutes before serving. Delicious with a seasonal salad for added crunch.

CALORIES	FAT	SAT FAT	PROTEIN	CARBS	SUGAR	SALT	FIBRE
771kcal	35.5g	16.7g	52.1g	57.4g	19.3g	1.8g	3g

David Tennant's

CROATIAN-STYLE CUTTLEFISH RISOTTO

WITH CHILLI-SPIKED PARSLEY OIL

· · · · · · · · · · · · · · · · SERVES 4 | TOTAL TIME – 1 HOUR · · · · · · · · · · · · · · · ·

David Tennant fell in love with this dish while filming in beautiful Dubrovnik back in 2004. Cooking risotto rice like this is really unusual, meaning you end up with more of a rice and seafood stew than a traditional risotto. Packed with incredible rich flavour and dark in colour, this is a treat for all the senses.

DAVID TENNANT'S CROATIAN-STYLE CUTTLEFISH RISOTTO
WITH CHILLI-SPIKED PARSLEY OIL

. . . .

1 x 1.2kg cuttlefish, cleaned, skin and trimmings reserved (500g total meat)

optional: 1 litre quality chicken stock

1 red onion

1 clove of garlic

½ a bunch of fresh flat-leaf parsley (15g)

3 large ripe tomatoes

olive oil

30g unsalted butter

3 anchovy fillets in oil

1 tablespoon tomato purée

50ml white wine

1 teaspoon cuttlefish ink

300g risotto rice

1 fresh red chilli

1 lemon

extra virgin olive oil

To make the fish stock, place the reserved cuttlefish skin and trimmings in a large pan. Pour in the chicken stock (if using) or 1 litre of boiling water and bring to the boil on a high heat. Simmer for 20 minutes, then strain through a fine sieve into another pan and leave over a very low heat to keep warm until needed.

Slice the tentacles from the cuttlefish, then open out the tubes and lightly score the underside in a criss-cross pattern with a regular eating knife. Chop it all into 2cm pieces. Peel the onion and garlic and finely chop on a clean board with the parsley stalks (reserving the leaves). Deseed and dice the tomatoes. Place a medium pan on a medium heat with 1 tablespoon of olive oil and the butter, then add the onion, garlic, parsley stalks and anchovies. Cook for 8 to 10 minutes, or until softened, stirring regularly. Add the cuttlefish, tomatoes, tomato purée, wine, cuttlefish ink and 500ml of stock. Cook for 15 minutes, or until the cuttlefish is tender. Meanwhile, cook the risotto rice in a pan of boiling salted water for 10 to 15 minutes, or until al dente, then drain.

Finely chop the parsley leaves, finely slice the chilli (deseed if you like), then, in a bowl, mix with most of the lemon juice and 1 tablespoon of extra virgin olive oil. Gently fold the drained rice into the cuttlefish pan and add a good squeeze of lemon juice. Remove from the heat and let it stand for 5 minutes so the rice sucks up some of that flavoursome liquid. Serve drizzled with the chilli-spiked parsley oil. Super-tasty!

CALORIES	FAT	SAT FAT	PROTEIN	CARBS	SUGAR	SALT	FIBRE
551kcal	14.6g	5.1g	35.2g	67.4g	7.8g	1.7g	2.8g

AMAZING RAVIOLI

RADICCHIO, BALSAMIC, POTATO & FONTINA

SERVES 6 | TOTAL TIME - 2 HOURS 45 MINUTES, PLUS COOLING

For me, this is both a pleasure to eat and a ritual to embrace – surrounding a wonderful filling with elegant, delicate pasta is definitely a skill worth learning. It's an incredible little parcel of deliciousness, and compared to the ravioli we grew up with, this filling of bitter-sweet chicory, melty cheese and potato is an absolute taste explosion for the palate.

¼ x Royal pasta dough
(see page 244)

fine semolina, for dusting

FILLING

1 radicchio or 2 red
chicory (150g in total)

1 large red onion

80ml balsamic vinegar

olive oil

1 bunch of fresh
thyme (30g)

300g Maris Piper potatoes

50g Parmesan cheese,
plus extra to serve

100g fontina cheese

75g blanched hazelnuts

40g unsalted butter

extra virgin olive oil

Preheat the oven to 200°C/400°F/gas 6. Start by making the Royal pasta dough (see page 244). While it rests, make the filling. Trim and quarter the radicchio, peel the onion and slice into eighths, then place in a small roasting tray. Pour over the balsamic and 2 tablespoons of olive oil, toss to coat, then strip over half the thyme leaves, reserving any pretty tips. Cover with a sheet of wet scrunched-up greaseproof paper and roast for 1 hour. Prick the potatoes and dry-roast in a separate tray alongside until cooked through, then remove. Once cool enough to handle, scoop the potatoes out of their skins and mash the insides in a bowl. Finely chop the radicchio and onion, then stir into the potato with 1 tablespoon of the balsamic juices from the tray. Finely grate in most of the Parmesan and all the fontina, mix well, then season to perfection with sea salt and black pepper. Leave to cool completely.

On a clean flour-dusted surface, roll out the pasta dough so it's 1mm thick and roughly 16cm wide (the width of a standard pasta machine) – see page 244 for extra instructions. Spoon heaped teaspoons of filling evenly down the pasta strips, slightly off centre, leaving a 5cm gap between each. Brush the exposed pasta lightly with water and fold the sheets in half over the filling. Gently seal around the filling, pushing out the air – you can cut them into 8cm circles with a pastry cutter or into squares with a knife. Place them on a semolina-dusted tray as you go – you'll get about 18 ravioli in total.

Toast the hazelnuts in a large frying pan on a medium heat until golden, then lightly brush and tip into a bowl. Cook the ravioli two portions at a time in a pan of boiling salted water for 3 to 4 minutes. Meanwhile, place the frying pan back on a low heat and add a splash of olive oil, a third of the butter, and a third of the remaining thyme leaves and tips. Fry until golden, then remove from the heat. Scoop the pasta straight into the buttery sauce, bringing some starchy cooking water with it, add a fine grating of Parmesan, toss gently, then spoon on to warmed plates. Finish each portion with a scattering of hazelnuts, a little extra virgin olive oil, some extra Parmesan and a few small drips of the balsamic juices, if you like. Serve up to your first lucky guests, while you crack on with the next two portions.

CALORIES	FAT	SAT FAT	PROTEIN	CARBS	SUGAR	SALT	FIBRE
479kcal	32.5g	10.9g	15.5g	32.1g	8g	0.5g	2.6g

ESSEX GUMBO

SURF 'N' TURF STEW

SERVES 10 | TOTAL TIME – 2 HOURS 10 MINUTES

A real melting pot of flavours, this delicious stew from the Deep South has African, French and Spanish influences. I've nicknamed it Essex gumbo, as this is my take on the classic – it's hearty, indulgent and a real flavour extravaganza.

200g quality chorizo

1 onion

3 sticks of celery

3 mixed-colour peppers

4 cloves of garlic

2 fresh mixed-colour chillies

2 medium sweet potatoes

4 sprigs of fresh rosemary

4 sprigs of fresh thyme

4 fresh bay leaves

1 teaspoon cayenne pepper

1 heaped tablespoon plain flour

1 x 400g tin of plum tomatoes

300g okra

300g white crabmeat

4 sprigs of fresh curly parsley

STOCK

1 x 1.6kg whole chicken, jointed, skin on, carcass reserved (ask your butcher)

olive oil

12 large raw shell-on tiger prawns

1 teaspoon cayenne pepper

1.5 litres quality chicken stock

PICKLED CHILLIES

6 fresh Scotch bonnet chillies

2 fresh bay leaves

extra virgin olive oil

white or red wine vinegar

To make the stock, put the chicken carcass into a large pan with a splash of olive oil, then place on a medium heat for 5 minutes, or until browned. Peel the prawns, adding the heads and shells to the pan. Add the cayenne and stock, bring to the boil, then simmer gently for 15 minutes.

Meanwhile, thickly slice the chorizo. Peel the onion and celery, deseed the peppers, then roughly chop. Peel the garlic, then finely slice with the chillies. Scrub the sweet potatoes and chop into 3cm chunks.

Place a large pan on a medium-high heat with 1 tablespoon of olive oil, the chorizo, rosemary and thyme sprigs, and 2 bay leaves. Cook for 5 minutes, or until browned, then remove everything to a plate. Generously season the chicken with sea salt and black pepper, then place in the pan, skin side down. Turn the heat up to high and cook for 10 minutes, or until browned, turning occasionally. Remove to a plate.

Add the chopped onion, celery, peppers, garlic and chillies to the pan with the cayenne and the remaining 2 bay leaves. Cook on a medium heat for 10 minutes, or until softened. Stir in the flour to coat, then sieve in 2 ladlefuls of the stock. Return the chicken and chorizo to the pan, along with the sweet potatoes and the tomatoes. Bring to the boil, breaking up the tomatoes with the back of a spoon. Cover and simmer for 40 minutes, or until the chicken is tender. Finely slice the Scotch bonnets (blanch them first in boiling water to reduce the heat, if you like). Bash the bay in a pestle and mortar with a pinch of salt, discarding the stalks. Muddle in a good lug of extra virgin olive oil and a splash of vinegar. Stir in the chopped chillies and set aside. Slice the okra and add to the gumbo pan for a further 10 minutes. Gently fold in the crabmeat and prawns for a final 5 minutes, or until cooked through. Season to perfection. Finely chop and scatter over the parsley, then serve with the pickled chillies. Good with brown rice and green salad.

CALORIES	FAT	SAT FAT	PROTEIN	CARBS	SUGAR	SALT	FIBRE
332kcal	12.2g	3.8g	36.2g	20.5g	9.4g	1.4g	4g

ROASTED GAME BIRD PIE

INCREDIBLE OLD-SCHOOL SUET PASTRY

• • • • • • • • • • SERVES 12 | TOTAL TIME – 5 HOURS 15 MINUTES • • • • • • • • • •

Have I got a pie for you! Start the story by roasting the birds, giving extra flavour, texture, and smiles all round – it's worth the wait. Add an aromatic herby hit, your low-and-slow veggie base, encase in beyond-delicious pastry, and you're on to a winner. All the leftover bones from the birds will make a brilliant stock.

ROASTED GAME BIRD PIE
INCREDIBLE OLD-SCHOOL SUET PASTRY

. . . .

1 x 1.4kg whole chicken

1 duck

1 pheasant

1 grouse

1 partridge

1 quail

½ a bunch of
  fresh thyme (15g)

½ a bunch of fresh
  rosemary (15g)

2 fresh bay leaves

1 tablespoon juniper
  berries

olive oil

1 red onion

3 carrots

2 sticks of celery

2 medium leeks

4 rashers of smoked
  streaky bacon

2 Maris Piper potatoes

1 litre quality chicken stock

2 tablespoons plain flour

500ml dry cider

PASTRY

600g plain flour,
  plus extra for dusting

150g shredded suet

150g unsalted butter (cold)

2 large eggs

Preheat the oven to 180°C/350°F/gas 4. Place all the birds in a large roasting tray. Strip the thyme and half the rosemary leaves into a pestle and mortar, then bash up with the bay, juniper berries, a pinch of sea salt and ½ a tablespoon of black pepper. Muddle in 6 tablespoons of oil, then rub all over the birds. Roast for 1 hour. Meanwhile, peel and finely chop the onion, carrots and celery. Wash, trim and finely slice the white part of the leeks (save the green for making stock or soup) and the bacon. Peel the potatoes and cut into 2cm chunks. Drizzle 1 tablespoon of oil into a large pan on a medium heat, add the bacon to render out the fat, then strip in the remaining rosemary. Once golden, add the onion, carrots, celery and leeks, then cook for 45 minutes on a medium-low heat, or until softened, stirring occasionally and adding the potatoes halfway through.

For the pastry, put the flour and a good pinch of salt into a bowl with the suet, cube and add the butter, then use your thumbs and forefingers to rub the fat into the flour until it resembles breadcrumbs. Beat the eggs, then, reserving just enough to eggwash the pie, stir into the bowl with 180ml of ice-cold water. Use your hands to gently bring it together into a ball, but don't overwork it. Wrap in clingfilm and chill in the fridge for at least 30 minutes.

When the time's up, remove the birds from the oven. When cool enough to handle, pick all the meat, discarding the skin and bones. Sieve the tray juices into the stock. Reduce the oven temperature to 170°C/325°F/gas 3. Stir the flour into the veg for 1 minute, then pour in the cider and cook for 10 minutes, or until slightly reduced. Shred the meat and stir into the veg pan, then add the stock. Season well, bring to the boil and simmer for 30 minutes, or until thickened. Carefully drain the liquid through a coarse sieve into a pan, skimming away any fat from the surface. Leave to cool.

Grease the bottom of a pie dish (25cm x 30cm) with a little oil. Roll out two-thirds of the pastry on a clean flour-dusted surface to ½cm thick and use it to line the pie dish. Stir 300ml of the strained gravy through the meat and spoon into the dish. Eggwash the edges. Roll out the remaining pastry to ½cm thick and a little bigger than the pie dish, then carefully place on top of the pie, trimming off any overhang. Pinch the edges to seal and make two small incisions in the centre for the steam to escape. Use any spare pastry to decorate the pie, if you like. Eggwash the top, then bake at the bottom of the oven for 1 hour, or until the pastry is golden and the pie is piping hot. To serve, reheat the remaining gravy, skimming off any fat from the surface, and serve alongside the pie. Delicious with creamy mashed potato and seasonal mustardy dressed greens.

CALORIES	FAT	SAT FAT	PROTEIN	CARBS	SUGAR	SALT	FIBRE
731kcal	41g	17.8g	37.6g	53.2g	5.4g	1g	3.7g

EMPIRE ROAST LAMB

MARINATED & SERVED WITH AN EPIC SAUCE

Sunday roast meets Friday night curry in this spectacular dish. Marinate the lamb in a wonderful mix of spices, then roast low and slow for tender meat that's gnarly, sticky and sweet. Serve on a platter of epic sauce – what's not to love?

1 x 2.5kg lamb shoulder, bone in

1 handful of curry leaves

olive oil

1 bunch of fresh coriander (30g)

extra virgin olive oil

MARINADE

5cm piece of ginger

1 bulb of garlic

1 large red onion

2 fresh green chillies

50g ground almonds

2 tablespoons fat-free natural yoghurt

1 tablespoon brown mustard seeds

1 tablespoon white wine vinegar

SAUCE

3cm piece of ginger

8 cloves of garlic

1 fresh green chilli

1 heaped tablespoon brown mustard seeds

1 handful of curry leaves

4 large ripe tomatoes

1 x 400g tin of light coconut milk

white wine vinegar or ½ a lemon

To make the marinade, peel the ginger, garlic and onion, and deseed the chillies. Place it all in a food processor with the rest of the marinade ingredients and blitz until smooth. Using a sharp knife, make about 10 incisions, roughly 4cm deep, all over the lamb, then poke a few curry leaves into each one. Sit the lamb in a snug-fitting roasting tray and massage half the marinade all over it. Pour the remainder around the lamb in the tray, then cover and marinate in the fridge for at least 2 hours, preferably overnight.

When ready to cook, preheat the oven to 220°C/425°F/gas 7 and remove the lamb from the fridge to come up to room temperature. Drizzle the lamb with olive oil and add a splash of water to the tray, then roast for 30 minutes. Reduce the oven temperature to 130°C/250°F/gas ½ and roast for a further 2 hours 30 minutes to 3 hours 30 minutes, or until the meat is tender and falls away from the bone. Remove the lamb to a board, cover with tin foil

and leave to rest for 15 minutes. Meanwhile, make the sauce. Peel the ginger and garlic, deseed the chilli, then finely slice it all. Transfer any excess fat from the roasting tray to a small jar to use another time, then place the tray over a medium heat on the hob. Stir in the mustard seeds and curry leaves for 1 minute, then add the ginger, garlic and chilli. Cook for 2 to 3 minutes, or until softened and lightly golden. Roughly chop and add the tomatoes, then stir in the coconut milk and simmer for a few minutes, or until thickened and reduced, stirring occasionally. Season to perfection with sea salt, black pepper and a splash of vinegar or a squeeze of lemon juice, then pour on to a large serving platter. Place the lamb on top, pick over the coriander leaves, drizzle with a little extra virgin olive oil, and place in the middle of the table, ready to be sliced and served. Good with all the trimmings – rice, chapattis or poppadoms and a fresh zingy salad.

CALORIES	FAT	SAT FAT	PROTEIN	CARBS	SUGAR	SALT	FIBRE
358kcal	26.3g	12g	25.3g	6.1g	3.2g	0.2g	1g

Anna Friel's
BALINESE PORK STEW

TURBOCHARGED WITH HOT CHILLI SAMBAL

•••••••••• SERVES 8 | TOTAL TIME – 2 HOURS 40 MINUTES ••••••••••

Anna tasted a stew like this while she was travelling in Bali in her early twenties, and has always wanted to try it again. The real hero here is the yellow curry paste – it's incredibly fragrant and definitely has a bit of a kick, but it also adds a gorgeous colour to the dish. Serve on a banana leaf to make this a total showstopper!

ANNA FRIEL'S BALINESE PORK STEW
TURBOCHARGED WITH HOT CHILLI SAMBAL

750g skinless boneless pork belly, cut into finger-length strips

750g pork ribs, halved

olive oil

300g Chinese long beans or green beans

300g pattypan squash

½ a Chinese cabbage

4 kaffir lime leaves

2 x 400g tins of light coconut milk

500g jasmine rice

4 limes

PASTE

20g fresh turmeric

80g galangal or ginger

400g small Thai shallots

1 bulb of garlic

2 fresh red bird's-eye chillies

3 fresh red chillies

5 candlenuts or macadamia nuts

1 tablespoon each of black and white peppercorns

50g palm sugar

1 teaspoon shrimp paste

SAMBAL

3 small Thai shallots

2 fresh red bird's-eye chillies

3 kaffir lime leaves

2 sticks of lemongrass

2 limes

coconut oil

Preheat the oven to 180°C/350°F/gas 4. To make the paste, peel and finely slice the fresh turmeric, then scrub and finely slice the galangal. Place in a dry frying pan for a few minutes, or until they start to release their oils, then turn the heat off. Peel and finely slice the shallots and garlic, then deseed and roughly chop all the chillies. Slice the nuts. Crush the peppercorns in a pestle and mortar, add all the other paste ingredients and a big pinch of sea salt, then bash and muddle everything together – work in batches, if you need to. Freeze half for another day.

Reserving 2 tablespoons of the remaining paste for later, place the rest in a large roasting tray. Add the meat and massage in all those lovely flavours. Drizzle with olive oil, then cover with a sheet of wet greaseproof paper and a layer of tin foil. Cook in the oven for 2 hours, or until beautifully browned and gnarly, shaking the tray halfway and removing the greaseproof and foil for the final 30 minutes.

Chop the Chinese long beans into 7cm chunks (if using), halve the squash across the middle, then roughly shred the cabbage. Remove the meat tray from the oven and place over a medium heat on the hob. Stir in the veg, lime leaves, reserved paste and coconut milk, and gently mix together. Bring to the boil, then simmer for 10 to 15 minutes, or until the veg are tender. Season to perfection.

Meanwhile, cook the rice according to the packet instructions, and prepare the sambal. Peel the shallots and finely slice with the chillies and lime leaves. Bash the lemongrass, remove and discard the outer layer, then finely slice. Mix it all in a small bowl with the lime juice and a drizzle of coconut oil, then season to perfection.

Dish up the rice and curry, and serve the sambal on the side, with lime wedges for squeezing over.

> I like to serve the stew on banana leaves. You can get them online or in good greengrocers' – they're pretty big, so you'll only need 2 or 3. Cut into pieces slightly larger than your bowls or plates, then hold them over the flame on your hob until bendy and pliable.

CALORIES	FAT	SAT FAT	PROTEIN	CARBS	SUGAR	SALT	FIBRE
709kcal	31.7g	15.4g	44.1g	61.9g	7.5g	0.5g	2.8g

CHICKEN IN A CRUST

HERBY MUSHROOM BUTTER

Cooking a whole chicken in a pastry crust will give you the most incredible flavour and beautifully tender results. It also looks brilliantly bonkers, so it makes the most fantastic centrepiece for a meal to impress your friends and family. Simply crack off and discard the crust, revealing that super-juicy bird hidden inside. Heaven.

20g dried porcini
   mushrooms

1 clove of garlic

120g wild mushrooms,
   such as chanterelles,
   girolles

olive oil

½ a bunch of fresh
   thyme (15g)

1 x 2.5kg whole chicken

2kg plain flour

½ a bunch of fresh
   flat-leaf parsley (15g)

truffle oil

170g unsalted butter
   (at room temperature)

In a small bowl, just cover the porcini with boiling water and leave to rehydrate for 10 minutes while you peel and finely slice the garlic and tear up the wild mushrooms. Place both in a frying pan on a medium heat with 1 tablespoon of olive oil. Strip in the thyme leaves and fry it all for 5 to 8 minutes, or until golden, stirring occasionally. Roughly chop the porcini and add to the pan, then pour in their soaking liquor (discarding just the last gritty bit). Cook for another 3 to 4 minutes, or until thickened and reduced, then season to perfection with sea salt and black pepper. Leave to cool.

Meanwhile, preheat the oven to 200°C/400°F/gas 6. Remove the chicken from the fridge and let it come up to room temperature. Place the flour in a bowl, then gradually pour in 1.2 litres of ice-cold water, stirring continuously until combined. Use your hands to bring it together into a soft, elastic dough, then cover with a damp tea towel and put aside.

Transfer the mushroom mixture to a board with the top leafy half of the parsley, add a few drops of truffle oil, then roughly chop together. Scrape into a bowl, then squidge and mix in the butter. Carefully lift up and push your fingers or a spoon between the chicken breast and skin on both sides of the bird to create pockets for your flavoured butter – be careful not to rip the skin. Rub most of the butter on to the breast meat, then replace the skin and massage the remaining butter all over. Tie the legs together with string.

Roll out one third of the dough into a rectangle 1cm thick and just slightly bigger than the chicken, then sit the chicken on top. Roll out the remainder of the dough to 1cm thick and big enough to cover the chicken. Place the dough over the top, pressing the edges together to create a sealed parcel. Place in a large roasting tray and cook in the oven for 1 hour 40 minutes – be exact with your timings, as you won't be able to check whether it's cooked until you carve the crust open.

Remove to a board to rest for 30 minutes, then break open the crust with a knife and discard (you don't eat the crust). Check that the chicken is cooked through, then carve it up and serve. Perfect with creamy mash and steamed seasonal greens.

CALORIES	FAT	SAT FAT	PROTEIN	CARBS	SUGAR	SALT	FIBRE
406kcal	30.8g	12.9g	30.5g	1.4g	0.3g	0.2g	0.6g

WHOLE RED SNAPPER

PUNCHY SALSA, BREADFRUIT BEIGNETS & PLANTAIN

½–1 Scotch bonnet chilli

¼ of a green pepper

3 cloves of garlic

2 spring onions

1 bunch each of fresh basil
and coriander (30g)

optional: 1 handful of
celery leaves

20g coconut oil

1 x 1kg red snapper, scaled,
cleaned, gutted

1 plantain

olive oil

½ a ripe avocado

SALSA

3 x ⅓ each of red, yellow
and green peppers

2 ripe plum tomatoes

½ a red onion

3 cloves of garlic

½ a cucumber

4 tablespoons white wine
vinegar

1 tablespoon West Indian
hot pepper sauce

BREADFRUIT BEIGNETS

½ a breadfruit (400g)

10g unsalted butter

75g panko breadcrumbs

750ml vegetable oil,
for frying

For the marinade, deseed the Scotch bonnet and pepper, peel the garlic, trim and quarter the spring onions, then place it all in a blender with the basil, half the coriander and the celery leaves (if using). Melt and add the coconut oil and whiz to a paste, loosening with a good splash of water, if needed. Use a sharp knife to score the fish all over on both sides, about 1cm deep. Rub over the marinade, getting it into all the slashes, then cover and marinate in the fridge for at least 4 hours.

For the salsa, deseed and finely chop the peppers. Cut a cross into the bottom of each tomato, plunge them into boiling water for 40 seconds, then peel away the skin. Peel the red onion and garlic, trim the cucumber, then finely chop it all with most of the remaining coriander, mixing as you go. Scrape into a bowl, stir in the vinegar and hot pepper sauce, then season to perfection with sea salt and black pepper.

To make the beignets, chop the breadfruit into large wedges and cook in boiling salted water with the lid ajar for 15 to 20 minutes, or until tender, then drain. Remove the skin and core, then mash while hot with the butter. Stir in 2 tablespoons of the salsa, then season to perfection. Divide the mixture into 20 balls, then roll them in the breadcrumbs and place on a tray. Put aside. Just under half fill a large sturdy pan with oil – the oil should be 8cm deep, but never fill your pan more than half full – and place on a medium-high heat. Use a thermometer to tell when it's ready (170°C), or add a piece of potato and wait until it turns golden – that's the sign that it's ready to go.

Meanwhile, preheat the oven to 220°C/425°F/gas 7, and preheat a large ovenproof frying pan or non-stick roasting tray on a high heat on the hob. Put in the snapper to char and colour for 2 minutes on each side, then transfer to the oven for 10 to 12 minutes, or until cooked through. To test if it's done, insert a small, sharp knife into the thickest part just behind the head – the fish should flake away. While it cooks, peel the plantain and halve lengthways. Drizzle 1 tablespoon of olive oil into a frying pan on a medium-high heat, and cook the plantain for 2 minutes on each side, or until golden. Season.

Carefully drop 6 beignets into the hot vegetable oil and cook for 2 to 3 minutes, or until golden, crisp and they rise to the surface. Scoop out and drain on kitchen paper (freeze the rest before frying, to defrost and cook fresh another day). Serve the fish with the salsa, beignets and plantain. Halve, destone and scoop over the avocado, and finish with a scattering of coriander leaves. Any leftover salsa will keep for up to 2 days in the fridge.

CALORIES	FAT	SAT FAT	PROTEIN	CARBS	SUGAR	SALT	FIBRE
789kcal	35.4g	13.4g	67g	53.7g	14.6g	2g	4.5g

Michael Sheen's
TRADITIONAL WELSH CAWL

HEARTY LAMB & ROOT VEG SOUP

•••••• SERVES 8 | TOTAL TIME – 1 HOUR 15 MINUTES, PLUS CHILLING ••••••

A total Welsh classic, this traditional dish reminds Michael of his grandmother's homely cooking. The ingredients are minimal, so it's worth giving a bit of love to prepping each veg to the perfect size so it's a pleasure to eat. To really bolster the flavours and let them develop, try making this the day before you need it.

MICHAEL SHEEN'S TRADITIONAL WELSH CAWL
HEARTY LAMB & ROOT VEG SOUP

1 onion

1kg lamb neck, bone in,
   cut into 5cm chunks
   (ask your butcher)

1kg swede

2 carrots

2 parsnips

500g Maris Piper potatoes

3 large leeks

mature Caerphilly cheese,
   to serve

Pour 2 litres of water into a large pan with 2 teaspoons of sea salt, then bring to the boil over a high heat. Peel and add the whole onion, along with the lamb. Bring back to the boil, skimming away any scum from the surface. Simmer on a medium heat for 10 to 15 minutes, or until the lamb is cooked through. Using a slotted spoon, remove the lamb to a plate and leave until cool enough to handle.

While it's cooling, peel the swede, chop into 1cm chunks, and add to the pan to get a headstart. Peel the carrots and parsnips, slice at a slight angle 1cm thick, and drop them into the pan. Now peel the potatoes and cut into 4cm chunks. Strip all the lamb meat from the bone, and return the meat to the pan with the potatoes. Bring back to the boil, then simmer it all for 15 to 20 minutes, or until almost tender, while you wash the leeks and cut them into 1cm-thick slices.

Now you can eat this straight away if you want to – simply stir the leeks into the pan, bring to the boil again, then simmer for 10 minutes with the lid on, or until tender. Taste and season to perfection. For even tastier results, let it chill overnight. In which case, simply stir in the raw leeks, cover, and pop into the fridge, where it will keep for up to 3 days. When you're ready to serve, gently simmer the cawl until warm through, then season. Either way, ladle into serving bowls and serve with lots of black pepper, a wedge of mature Caerphilly cheese and a slice of good bread and butter for dunking.

CALORIES	FAT	SAT FAT	PROTEIN	CARBS	SUGAR	SALT	FIBRE
379kcal	18.6g	8.1g	28.1g	26.1g	12.1g	1.3g	6.7g

ARROSTO MISTO

OOZY POLENTA & GREMOLATA

• • • • • • • • • SERVES 14 | TOTAL TIME – 2 HOURS 30 MINUTES • • • • • • • • •

This Italian blockbuster Sunday roast is a real celebration of a dish – five birds and one sausage wheel, all piled on to deliciously cheesy polenta. It's certainly epic, but if you're after a super-special showstopper, it's guaranteed to please.

ARROSTO MISTO
OOZY POLENTA & GREMOLATA

. . . .

1 bulb of garlic

½ a bunch of fresh thyme (15g)

olive oil

1 x 1.8kg whole chicken

1 lemon

1 x 2kg whole duck

1 stick of cinnamon

½ a bunch of fresh sage (15g)

4 bulbs of fennel

6 red onions

2 long sturdy sprigs of fresh rosemary

2 pigeons

2 partridges

2 quails

500g quality sausages, in one string

8 fresh bay leaves

1 tablespoon plain flour

150ml Chianti, or other red wine

1 x 400g tin of quality plum tomatoes

300ml quality chicken stock

GREMOLATA

2 cloves of garlic

½ a bunch of fresh
    flat-leaf parsley (15g)

1 lemon

POLENTA

250g coarse polenta

100g unsalted butter

150g Parmesan cheese

Preheat the oven to full whack (240°C/475°F/gas 9). Peel 3 cloves of garlic and bash well in a pestle and mortar with half the thyme leaves and a good pinch of sea salt and black pepper, then muddle in a good splash of oil. Rub all over the chicken, getting into all the nooks and crannies. Halve the lemon and place in the cavity with the remaining thyme sprigs. Season the duck all over, rub with a good drizzle of oil, then finely grate over half the cinnamon stick. Place the rest of the stick in the cavity with the sage.

Reserving the herby tops, trim and halve the fennel, then place in a large roasting tray with the whole, unpeeled onions and the remaining garlic cloves. Sit the chicken and duck on the top shelf of the oven, directly on the bars, with the fennel tray underneath. Turn the temperature down to 180°C/350°F/gas 4 and cook for 1 hour 30 minutes, or until the chicken is tender and the juices run clear.

Pick the leaves from the rosemary sprigs into the pestle and mortar, then bash and bruise with a good splash of oil. Season the pigeons, partridges and quails all over, then drizzle with the rosemary oil. Gently untwist the links

between the sausages and push the meat along to make one giant sausage. Start curling one end in, then twirl the sausage round itself until you have one big spiral of sausage, poking in the bay leaves. Sharpen the ends of the rosemary sprigs, then use them to skewer and secure the sausages in place. Drizzle with oil.

Once the chicken is cooked, remove to a plate, cover with tin foil and a clean tea towel, then leave to rest. Place the rest of the birds directly on the oven shelf next to the duck. Sit the sausage wheel on top of the veg in the tray, then cook it all for 30 minutes, or until the birds are tender and cooked through. Meanwhile, to make the gremolata, peel the garlic, finely chop with the parsley leaves, then place in a bowl with the reserved fennel tops. Finely grate over the lemon zest, add a squeeze of juice and mix well.

Remove the cooked birds from the oven and leave to rest. Move the roasting tray to the top shelf for a further 15 minutes, or until the sausage is cooked through and golden. Meanwhile, bring 1.1 litres of water to the boil in a large pan, then gradually add the polenta, whisking continuously

CALORIES	FAT	SAT FAT	PROTEIN	CARBS	SUGAR	SALT	FIBRE
593kcal	30.3g	12g	57.4g	20.7g	2.8g	1.2g	3.2g

until combined. Continue to stir over the heat for 15 to 20 minutes, or until oozy, thick and smooth.

Transfer the cooked veggies and sausage wheel to a plate, then skim away and discard the fat from the tray. Place on a medium heat on the hob, stir in the flour for 1 minute, then pour in the Chianti. Scrape up all that goodness from the bottom of the tray, then add the plum tomatoes, any resting juices from the chicken and the stock. Bring to the boil, then simmer for 5 minutes, or until thickened and reduced to a lovely gravy consistency.

Stir the butter into the polenta and finely grate in the Parmesan, loosening with a little water, if needed. Season to taste. Carve up the birds and slice the sausage, squeeze the onions and garlic out of their skins, then serve it all up on a board with the polenta. Scatter over the gremolata and serve the gravy and some steamed greens on the side.

SALMON EN CROÛTE

SPINACH-STUFFED CRUST & CHEESY SAUCE

SERVES 8 | TOTAL TIME – 1 HOUR AND 10 MINUTES, PLUS COOLING

I couldn't resist the opportunity to go a bit retro and include my version of salmon en croûte – it's such a nostalgic dish for many of us, and making it yourself is not only super-satisfying, it creates a brilliantly exciting centrepiece.

2 onions

2 cloves of garlic

olive oil

50g unsalted butter

½ a bunch of fresh oregano (15g)

1kg frozen chopped spinach

375g all-butter puff pastry (cold)

1 x 1kg side of salmon, skin off, pin-boned (ask your fishmonger for a fillet from the top end of the fish)

1 large egg

SAUCE

1 leek

50g sun-dried tomatoes

100ml white wine

1 tablespoon plain flour, plus extra for dusting

250ml semi-skimmed milk

50g Red Leicester cheese

cayenne pepper

Peel and finely slice the onions and garlic, then place in a large pan on a medium heat with 1 tablespoon of oil and half the butter. Pick in the oregano leaves and cook for 10 minutes, stirring regularly. Add the spinach and cook for a further 15 to 20 minutes, or until the liquid has evaporated, still stirring regularly. Remove from the heat, taste, season to perfection with sea salt and black pepper and allow to cool.

Meanwhile, make the sauce: wash, trim and finely slice the leek, then place in a large pan on a medium-low heat with 1 tablespoon of oil, the remaining butter and the sun-dried tomatoes. Cook for 15 minutes, or until sweet and tender, stirring regularly. Pour in the wine and let it bubble and cook away, then stir in the flour and, splash by splash, stir in the milk. Leave it to simmer for 5 minutes, then liquidize in a blender until silky smooth. Grate in the cheese, add a pinch of cayenne and blitz again to combine. Taste and season to perfection, then leave to cool completely.

Preheat the oven to 220°C/425°F/gas 7 and place a large baking sheet inside to heat up. On a large sheet of flour-dusted greaseproof paper, roll out the pastry so it's 10cm bigger than your salmon all the way round. Pour away any excess liquid from the cooled spinach mixture, then spoon it on to the middle of the pastry and spread it across the surface, leaving a 3cm border at the edges. Place the salmon in the middle, then roll up the sides of the pastry to create the crust, going right up to the salmon and pinching it at the corners to secure it in place. Lightly score the top of the salmon in a criss-cross fashion, then pour the cool cheesy sauce over the fish. Brush the exposed pastry with beaten egg, then carefully lift the greaseproof and salmon en croûte on to the preheated tray. Bake at the bottom of the oven for 30 to 40 minutes, or until golden and cooked through. This is delicious served with a garden salad and lemon wedges on the side for squeezing over.

CALORIES	FAT	SAT FAT	PROTEIN	CARBS	SUGAR	SALT	FIBRE
657kcal	43.5g	14.8g	37.3g	36.7g	7.1g	1.1g	2.9g

Dexter Fletcher's
PARTY-TIME
MEXICAN TACOS

TENDER CHICKEN, ZINGY SALSA, FETA & SEEDS

SERVES 16 | TOTAL TIME - 2 HOURS

I made these tacos for my good friend, actor and director, Dexter, who first fell in love with tacos on a trip to Playa del Carmen in Mexico. Shredded roast chicken and all the trimmings, stuffed into homemade tortillas with a drizzle of super-fresh, zingy, spicy salsa – this epic taco recipe is perfect when entertaining a crowd.

DEXTER FLETCHER'S PARTY-TIME MEXICAN TACOS

TENDER CHICKEN, ZINGY SALSA, FETA & SEEDS

- -

1 x 1.8kg whole chicken

4 sprigs of fresh thyme

olive oil

1 lemon

1 bulb of garlic

500g plain flour,
  plus extra for dusting

1 cos lettuce

250g ripe cherry tomatoes

2 ripe avocados

100g mixed seeds

200g feta cheese

SALSA

2 fresh red or green chillies

500g tomatillos or green
  tomatoes

1 bunch of fresh mint (30g)

1 bunch of fresh
  coriander (30g)

2 spring onions

1 clove of garlic

2 tablespoons cider vinegar

2 extra virgin olive oil

1 splash of quality tequila

Get the chicken out of the fridge and up to room temperature before you cook it. Preheat the oven to 180°C/350°F/gas 4. Strip the thyme leaves into a pestle and mortar and pound with a good pinch of sea salt and black pepper, then rub all over the chicken with 1 tablespoon of olive oil. Halve the lemon, bash the garlic bulb, discarding the outer skin, then stuff inside the chicken cavity. Sit the bird in a snug-fitting roasting tray and roast for around 1 hour 30 minutes, or until cooked through. To check, insert a knife into the thickest part of the thigh – if the juices run clear, you know it's done.

Meanwhile, place the flour and a pinch of salt in a large bowl, then gradually add 2 tablespoons of olive oil and 150ml of ice-cold water, stirring continuously until the mixture forms a rough dough. Knead on a clean flour-dusted surface for around 5 minutes, or until smooth and elastic, then shape into a long sausage, roughly 45cm in length. Slice into 16 equal-sized pieces, roll into balls, and set aside for later.

To make the salsa, preheat a griddle pan over a high heat. Prick the chillies with a small sharp knife, peel back the papery skin from the tomatillos, then place on the griddle. Cook for 10 minutes, or until gnarly and bar-marked, turning occasionally, while you pick half the mint leaves into a food processor with half the coriander (stalks and all). Trim and add the spring onions, peel and add the garlic clove, then add the chillies, tomatillos (discard the papery skin), vinegar, 2 tablespoons of extra virgin olive oil, the tequila and a good pinch of salt. Blitz until smooth.

Once cooked, allow the chicken to cool slightly, then strip away the meat, shredding it as you go. On a clean flour-dusted surface, roll the dough balls into circles, roughly the thickness of a playing card. Preheat a large non-stick frying pan over a high heat, then, in batches, cook the tortillas for 2 to 3 minutes, or until lightly golden, turning halfway. Wrap in tin foil as you go to keep warm. Meanwhile, shred the lettuce, quarter the cherry tomatoes, then halve and destone the avocados. Pick the remaining herb leaves.

Serve everything in the middle of the table with the mixed seeds and feta, and let everyone tuck in and build their own tacos. Delicious with a squeeze of lime juice.

CALORIES	FAT	SAT FAT	PROTEIN	CARBS	SUGAR	SALT	FIBRE
429kcal	23.9g	5.5g	22.1g	33.3g	3.4g	2.2g	3.8g

Orlando Bloom's
LAMB SHANK TAGINE

ZINGY FRESH HERB & OLIVE SALAD

· · · · · · · · · · SERVES 4 | TOTAL TIME – 3 HOURS 20 MINUTES · · · · · · · · · ·

Orlando has spent a lot of time filming in Morocco, so I've put together this recipe in his honour. Melt-in-the-mouth lamb is the star, but this dish celebrates some amazing veggies, too. Big, rich, spiced sweet and savoury flavours, with little punches of warm heat all in one bowl – this is next-level food. Love it!

ORLANDO BLOOM'S LAMB SHANK TAGINE

ZINGY FRESH HERB & OLIVE SALAD

4 lamb shanks, French trimmed

olive oil

1 fresh red chilli

1 clove of garlic

1 red onion

1 quince

2 carrots

1 bulb of fennel

2 fresh bay leaves

1 pinch of saffron

2 ripe tomatoes, on the vine

1 preserved lemon

1 litre quality chicken stock

200g couscous

1 bunch of fresh mint (30g)

1 handful of black olives (stone in)

½ a bunch of fresh
  flat-leaf parsley (15g)

½ a lemon

½ an orange

extra virgin olive oil

50g rose harissa

4 heaped tablespoons fat-free
  natural yoghurt

RAS EL HANOUT

2 cardamom pods

½ teaspoon ground cinnamon

1 teaspoon cayenne pepper

1 heaped teaspoon coriander seeds

½ teaspoon sweet smoked paprika

1 tiny pinch of cumin seeds

½ teaspoon ground turmeric

½ teaspoon ground ginger

Preheat the oven to 160°C/325°F/gas 3. To make the ras el hanout, lightly bash the cardamom pods in a pestle and mortar, then shake out the seeds, discarding the pods. Bash and muddle in the remaining ingredients to form a powder. Massage into the lamb shanks, then place in a large ovenproof pan on a medium-high heat with ½ a tablespoon of olive oil. Cook for 6 to 8 minutes, or until browned all over, turning regularly. Prick the chilli and add alongside the lamb until slightly scalded all over, then remove both lamb and chilli to a plate.

Peel and finely slice the garlic. Peel the onion and quince, cutting each into 8 wedges. Peel the carrots and chop at an angle into 4cm chunks. Trim and quarter the fennel bulb. Wipe out the pan with a ball of kitchen paper, then place on a medium heat with ½ a tablespoon of olive oil, the pricked chilli, bay leaves, garlic, quince and veg. Cook for 10 to 12 minutes, or until softened, stirring occasionally. In a cup, just cover the saffron with boiling water.

Return the lamb shanks to the pan, then quarter and add the tomatoes along with the saffron mixture, whole preserved lemon and stock. Bring to the boil. Cover the surface with a scrunched-up circular sheet of wet greaseproof paper, then pop a lid on. Cook in the oven for 2 hours to 2 hours 30 minutes, or until the shanks are soft and delicious and the sauce has reduced. Use a spoon to skim away any excess fat from the surface, then carefully remove the shanks to a plate. Place the pan on a medium-high heat for 5 to 10 minutes, or until the sauce has thickened and reduced, stirring occasionally.

Place the couscous and half the mint sprigs in a bowl, just cover with boiling water, pop a plate on top and leave to soak and infuse. To make a salad, destone the olives and roughly tear into a bowl. Pick in the parsley and remaining mint leaves, squeeze over the lemon and orange juice, add a drizzle of extra virgin olive oil and a pinch of sea salt and black pepper, then toss together. Swirl the harissa through the yoghurt. Return the lamb shanks to the sauce.

Fluff up the couscous, discarding the mint, then divide between your plates. Spoon over the tagine, sprinkle over the salad, and finish with a dollop of harissa yoghurt.

CALORIES	FAT	SAT FAT	PROTEIN	CARBS	SUGAR	SALT	FIBRE
881kcal	43.9g	15.3g	83.8g	40.6g	12.7g	1.6g	4.9g

LUXURIOUS FISH PIE
CREAMY PROSECCO SAUCE & RED LEICESTER MASH

In the UK, we are lucky enough to have access to the most wonderful changing bounty of gorgeous fish, from cold, clean glorious waters. This dish is a total classic that celebrates them all – please vary your fish choices according to what's available locally, and at its best. For me, this pie is particularly special made around Christmas.

1 x 1.5kg whole live lobster

600ml semi-skimmed milk

1 onion

1 large carrot

1 bulb of fennel

1 leek

olive oil

50g unsalted butter

2 tablespoons plain flour

2 teaspoons English
   mustard

150ml Prosecco

50g Lancashire or Cheddar
   cheese

2kg Maris Piper potatoes

75g Red Leicester cheese

cayenne pepper

200g seasonal greens,
   such as kale, cavolo
   nero, chard

1kg mixed fish fillets and
   seafood, such as smoked
   haddock, scallops,
   salmon, bass, gurnard,
   lemon sole, skin off,
   pin-boned

10 raw peeled king prawns

Buy your lobster on the day you want to cook it. Ask your fishmonger to kill it for you, or if you're happy doing it yourself, place the live lobster in the freezer for 30 minutes, so it's docile. When ready to cook, carefully and swiftly place the lobster in a large pan of boiling water head first, pop the lid on and cook for 8 minutes. Remove, cool, and carefully halve the lobster, then remove the meat to a bowl – save the claws to decorate, if you like, or, even better, crack, pull out the meat and add it to the bowl. Put all the shells back into the empty pan you cooked the lobster in and bash with a rolling pin, then pour in the milk and simmer on a low heat for 15 to 20 minutes to impart unbelievable flavour.

Meanwhile, peel the onion and carrot, trim the fennel, wash the leek, finely chop it all and place in a large casserole pan on a medium heat with 1 tablespoon of oil and half the butter. Cook for 15 minutes, or until soft and sticky, stirring regularly. Stir in the flour, followed by the mustard and Prosecco. Let the alcohol bubble and cook away, then strain and gradually stir in the milk and simmer until you have a nice, loose, silky consistency. Remove from the heat, grate in the Lancashire cheese, taste, season to perfection with sea salt and black pepper and leave to cool.

Peel the potatoes, cutting up any larger ones so they're all a similar size, then cook in a large pan of boiling salted water for 15 to 20 minutes, or until cooked through. Drain in a colander and leave to steam dry, then return to the pan and mash well with the remaining butter and the grated Red Leicester. Season to perfection with sea salt and cayenne, loosening with a splash of milk, if needed. Preheat the oven to 180°C/350°F/gas 4.

Remove any tough stalks from the greens, then finely chop and sprinkle into a baking dish (30cm x 35cm). Slice all the fish into bite-sized pieces and add to the dish, halve and add the prawns (deveining, if needed), then dot the lobster meat in and around. Pour over the sauce, top with the mash, then drizzle lightly with oil and poke in your lobster claws (if using). Bake for 1 hour, or until golden, bubbling and the fish is cooked through.

CALORIES	FAT	SAT FAT	PROTEIN	CARBS	SUGAR	SALT	FIBRE
510kcal	18.8g	7.4g	40.6g	45.6g	7.6g	1g	4.8g

Salma Hayek's
LEBANESE KIBBEH

AMBA SAUCE & SILKY HOUMOUS

• • • • • • • • • • • SERVES 6-8 | TOTAL TIME - 1 HOUR 45 MINUTES • • • • • • • • • • •

Inspired by a family trip Salma made to Lebanon, this is a celebratory twist on a delicious Lebanese national dish. These mini meaty croquettes are brimming with gorgeous Middle Eastern flavours, and there's a beautiful hint of sweetness from the dates that really cuts through the spices, adding an extra flavour dimension.

SALMA HAYEK'S LEBANESE KIBBEH
AMBA SAUCE & SILKY HOUMOUS

vegetable oil, for
  deep-frying

KIBBEH DOUGH

200g fine bulgur wheat

300g minced lamb
  (20% fat)

1 large pinch of
  seven-spice (see right)

½ tablespoon ghee

SEVEN-SPICE

½ tablespoon ground
  allspice

½ tablespoon ground
  cinnamon

½ teaspoon ground
  nutmeg

½ teaspoon ground
  coriander

½ teaspoon ground cloves

½ teaspoon ground ginger

½ teaspoon freshly
  ground black pepper

FILLING

50g pickled walnuts

50g Medjool dates

½ a bunch of fresh flat-leaf
  parsley (15g)

olive oil

200g minced lamb
  (20% fat)

50g pine nuts

2 teaspoons seven-spice
  (see left)

½ teaspoon dried mint

½ teaspoon dried oregano

In a bowl, cover the bulgur wheat with 200ml of cold water, then leave to soak for about 15 minutes. Mix the seven-spice ingredients together (it'll make more than you need, but save the rest in an airtight jar for another day).

For the filling, finely chop the walnuts, destone and roughly chop the dates, and finely chop the top leafy half of the parsley. Place a large frying pan on a high heat with ½ a tablespoon of olive oil, the minced lamb, pine nuts and walnuts. Cook for 5 to 10 minutes, or until starting to crisp up, stirring occasionally. Add 2 teaspoons of the seven-spice and the dried herbs, then cook for a further 5 minutes, or until dark golden and gnarly. Leave to cool, then stir through the chopped parsley.

Drain the bulgur (if needed), and mix with the remaining kibbeh dough ingredients and a good pinch of sea salt until it comes together – this will become your outer layer. Divide the mixture into 16 balls (roughly 50g each). Place one ball on the palm of your hand, then press and flatten into an oval shape, roughly 7cm x 8cm. Place a good pinch

of cooled filling into the centre, then mould the dough up and around the filling to seal. Repeat with the remaining ingredients, then place in the fridge to firm up for around 30 minutes. Now's a good time to get on with making the Amba sauce and Houmous (see page 243).

When you're ready to cook, just under half fill a large sturdy pan with oil – the oil should be 8cm deep, but never fill your pan more than half full – and place on a medium-high heat. Use a thermometer to tell when it's ready (170°C), or add a piece of potato and wait until it turns golden – that's the sign that it's ready to go. Carefully lower one kibbeh into the pan – after 3½ to 4 minutes it should be golden and perfectly cooked through, so take it out of the pan and cut it in half to check your timings – once you know where you stand, you can cook the rest, in batches.

Serve the kibbeh with the houmous and amba sauce. It's also good with pickled veg, flatbreads and a sprinkling of pomegranate seeds and fresh herbs.

CALORIES	FAT	SAT FAT	PROTEIN	CARBS	SUGAR	SALT	FIBRE
556kcal	40g	8.9g	22.4g	29.5g	3.6g	0.5g	2.5g

AMBA SAUCE

BLENDED MANGO, GARLIC & SPICES

· SERVES 6-8 | TOTAL TIME - 5 MINUTES, PLUS COOLING · · · · · · · · · · · · · · · · · · ·

Take your kibbeh to the next level with this quick and easy sauce that I just love. It's fresh and zingy, it's simple, and it's totally delicious. I know you'll love it, too. Give it a go.

1 ripe mango

1 large or 2 small limes

1 clove of garlic

olive oil

¼ teaspoon mustard seeds

¼ teaspoon fenugreek seeds

¼ teaspoon cayenne pepper

¼ teaspoon sweet smoked paprika

¼ teaspoon ground turmeric

optional: 1 pinch of cayenne pepper

Peel and destone the mango, then put the flesh into a blender. Finely grate in the lime zest, squeeze in the juice and blitz until smooth. Peel and finely slice the garlic, then place in a frying pan on a medium heat with ½ a tablespoon of olive oil and all the spices. Toast until lightly golden, then stir in the blitzed mango. Season to perfection, then leave to cool.

CALORIES	FAT	SAT FAT	PROTEIN	CARBS	SUGAR	SALT	FIBRE
26kcal	1.3g	0.2g	0.4g	3.8g	3.5g	0g	0.1g

HOUMOUS

SMOOTH & DELICIOUS

· SERVES 6-8 | TOTAL TIME - 5 MINUTES ·

Houmous is a really important part of Middle Eastern food and is ridiculously easy to make from scratch. Have a go at home and experience the joy of homemade houmous. Seriously good!

1 x 700g jar of quality chickpeas

1 lemon

1 clove of garlic

1 good pinch of ground cumin

2 tablespoons tahini

extra virgin olive oil

Pour the chickpeas (juice and all) into a blender and squeeze in the lemon juice. Peel and add the garlic, along with the cumin, a good pinch of sea salt, the tahini and a good lug of extra virgin olive oil. Blitz until creamy, then season to perfection, loosening with a little extra oil, if needed.

CALORIES	FAT	SAT FAT	PROTEIN	CARBS	SUGAR	SALT	FIBRE
131kcal	7.6g	1.1g	5.4g	10.5g	0.4g	0.3g	3.6g

ROYAL PASTA DOUGH

FOR THE SILKIEST VELVETY PASTA

SERVES 8 | TOTAL TIME - 30 MINUTES, PLUS RESTING

Made with a simple blend of Tipo 00 flour (00 means it's super-fine) and fine semolina, which has wonderful flavour and a golden colour, as well as free-range egg yolks, this is my ultimate fresh pasta dough recipe.

400g Tipo 00 flour,
  plus extra for dusting

75g fine semolina

12 large eggs

2 tablespoons extra virgin
  olive oil

THE DOUGH Pile the flour and semolina into a large bowl and make a well in the middle. Separate the eggs and add the yolks to the well (freeze the egg whites for making meringues another day). Add the extra virgin olive oil and 4 tablespoons of cold water to the well, use a fork to whip up with the yolks until smooth, then gradually bring the flour in from the outside until it becomes too hard to mix. Get your floured hands in there and bring it together into a ball of dough, then knead on a clean flour-dusted surface for 4 minutes, or until smooth and elastic (eggs can vary in size and flour can vary in humidity; this dough shouldn't be too wet or dry, but tweak with a touch more water or flour if you need to – use your common sense). Wrap in clingfilm and leave to relax for 30 minutes.

ROLLING OUT Divide your pasta dough into 4 pieces, covering everything with a clean damp tea towel as you go to stop it drying out. You can roll it out to your desired thickness with a rolling pin, but I think it's more accurate and fun to use a pasta machine, in which case attach it firmly to a clean table.

STAGE 1 One at a time, flatten each piece of dough by hand and run it through the thickest setting, then take the rollers down two settings and run the dough through again to make it thinner. Importantly, fold it in half and run it back through the thickest setting again – I like to repeat this a few times because it makes the dough super-smooth and turns it from a tatty sheet into one that fills out the pasta machine properly.

STAGE 2 Start rolling the sheet down through each setting, dusting with flour as you go. Turn the crank with one hand while the other maintains just a little tension to avoid any kinks, folds or ripples. On a clean flour-dusted surface, take it right down to the desired thickness. Generally speaking you want about 2mm for shapes like linguine, tagliatelle and lasagne, then to go as thin as 1mm for anything turned into a filled pasta, because when it's folded around a filling it will double up to 2mm. And remember, some shapes are easier than others, but with a bit of patience and practice, you'll soon get the hang of it.

CALORIES	FAT	SAT FAT	PROTEIN	CARBS	SUGAR	SALT	FIBRE
346kcal	14.3g	3.6g	12.3g	42.4g	0.7g	0.1g	1.7g

A NOTE FROM JAMIE'S NUTRITION TEAM

'Our job is to make sure that Jamie can be super-creative, while also ensuring that all his recipes meet the guidelines we set. Every book has a different brief, and, by nature, most of the recipes in *Jamie's Friday Night Feast Cookbook* are indulgent, therefore not to be enjoyed every day – they're a real celebration of weekend and special occasion cooking. So that you can make clear, informed choices, we've published the nutritional content for each recipe on the actual recipe page itself, giving you a really easy access point to understand how to fit these recipes into your week. You know the score – a good, balanced, varied diet and regular exercise are the keys to a healthier lifestyle. For more info about how we analyse recipes, please visit jamieoliver.com/nutrition.'

Rozzie Batchelar, Senior Nutritionist, RNutr (food)

FOOD STANDARDS

I think there's no point in eating meat unless the animal was raised well, was free to roam, lived in an unstressful environment and was in great health. It makes total sense that what we put into our bodies is optimal in every way, to in turn give us maximum goodness.

I also think that we should all be striving to eat more plant-based meals that hero veg, beans and pulses, and enjoying better-quality meat, less often. With this in mind, please choose organic, free-range or higher-welfare meat whenever you can, making sure beef or lamb is grass-fed. The same goes for eggs and anything containing eggs, such as pasta – choose free-range or organic, and please choose organic stock.

When it comes to buying fish, make sure you choose responsibly sourced wherever possible – look for the MSC logo, or talk to your fishmonger or the guys at the fish counter in your local supermarket and take their advice. Try to mix up your choices, choosing seasonal, sustainable options as they're available.

With staple dairy products, like milk, yoghurt and butter, I couldn't encourage you more to trade-up to organic whenever possible. It is slightly more expensive, but we're talking pennies not pounds, so this is a much easier trade-up than with meat. Plus, every time you buy organic, you are voting for a better food system.

A NOTE ON FREEZING

Let food cool before freezing, breaking it down into portions so it cools quicker and you can get it into the freezer within 2 hours of cooking. Make sure everything is well wrapped, meat and fish especially, and labelled for future reference. Thaw in the fridge before use. Generally, if you've frozen cooked food, don't freeze it again after you've reheated it.

Hungry for more?

For handy nutrition advice and loads of brilliant recipes, as well as videos, features,
hints, tricks and tips on all sorts of different subjects, plus much more, check out

JAMIEOLIVER.COM

Index

Recipes marked V are suitable for vegetarians

Books by Jamie Oliver

MICHAEL JOSEPH

UK | USA | CANADA | IRELAND | AUSTRALIA | INDIA | NEW ZEALAND | SOUTH AFRICA

Michael Joseph is part of the Penguin Random House group of companies,
whose addresses can be found at global.penguinrandomhouse.com

Penguin
Random House
UK

First published 2018

001

Copyright © Jamie Oliver, 2018

Photography copyright © Jamie Oliver Enterprises Limited, 2018

Photography by David Loftus: front (2) / back (3) cover and pages 4–5, 6, 24, 25, 27, 29, 31, 40, 43, 53, 55, 95, 102, 103, 105, 121, 136, 137, 139, 145, 146, 147, 149, 167, 171, 173, 174–5, 177, 178, 183, 211, 217, 229, 239, 241 & 245; Steve Ryan: back (5) cover and pages 9, 10, 13 (bottom), 15, 17, 21, 22 (bottom), 41, 48, 51, 56–7, 60, 63, 64, 67, 68, 71, 77, 82, 85, 89, 93 (top r./bottom l.), 97, 101, 107, 113, 115, 117, 119 (l./r.), 122, 125, 126–7, 129 (4), 130, 133, 135, 151, 152, 155, 165, 166, 169, 184, 187, 191, 197, 202–3, 205, 207, 209 (4), 215, 223, 225, 227, 233, 237, 247 & 256; Ella Miller: front (3) / back (4) cover and pages 11, 13 (top), 19, 22 (top 2), 32–3, 35, 37, 39 (4), 44–5, 47, 49, 59, 61, 65, 69, 73, 74–5, 83, 87, 91, 93 (top l./bottom r.), 109, 111, 123, 131, 140–41, 143, 158–9, 161 (2), 163, 179 (4), 185, 188 (2), 193, 195, 198–9, 201, 219 & 221; Joe Sarah: pages 79, 99, 153 & 157; James Lyndsay: pages 217, 231 & 235. Every effort has been made to ensure images are correctly attributed; however, if any omission or error has been made please notify the publisher for correction in future editions.

Design by Superfantastic

Colour reproduction by Altaimage Ltd

Printed in Germany by Mohn Media

A CIP catalogue record for this book is available from the British Library

ISBN: 978–0–241–37144–2

penguin.co.uk

jamieoliver.com

www.greenpenguin.co.uk

MIX
Paper from
responsible sources
FSC® C018179

Penguin Random House is committed to a sustainable future for our business, our readers and our planet. This book is made from Forest Stewardship Council® certified paper.